CELEBRATE
YOUR BODY
(AND ITS CHANGES, TOO!)

THE ULTIMATE PUBERTY BOOK FOR GIRLS

CELEBRATE YOUR BODY

(and Its Changes, Too!)

SONYA RENEE TAYLOR

Foreword by **BIANCA I. LAUREANO**
Illustrated by **CAIT BRENNAN**

ROCKRIDGE
PRESS

For general information on our other products and services or to obtain technical support, please contact our Customer Care Department within the United States at (866) 744-2665, or outside the United States at (510) 253-0500.

Rockridge Press publishes its books in a variety of electronic and print formats. Some content that appears in print may not be available in electronic books, and vice versa.

TRADEMARKS: Rockridge Press and the Rockridge Press logo are trademarks or registered trademarks of Callisto Media Inc. and/or its affiliates, in the United States and other countries, and may not be used without written permission. All other trademarks are the property of their respective owners. Rockridge Press is not associated with any product or vendor mentioned in this book.

Illustration © Cait Brennan, 2018

ISBN: Print 978-1-64152-166-6 | eBook 978-1-64152-028-7

R1

Printed in Canada

This book is dedicated to my cousin Nyah. May you, and every girl, grow up in a world where you are able to celebrate your glorious body without apology!

CONTENTS

FOREWORD

THERE ARE ONLY A FEW GUARANTEES IN THIS LIFE, and one of them is change! Change is happening right now all over the world, and it's happening right now in our bodies.

Sonya Renee Taylor has written a book for young girls who are experiencing the changes in their body that happen during puberty. Often these conversations are stale and clinical, but not here.

In *Celebrate Your Body (and Its Changes, Too!)* you will find all the important, practical medical information about puberty—but here it is combined with a new understanding of the fantastic shift that your body experiences during this time. Sonya answers questions you may not realize you have, or questions you have but don't know how to ask. You'll read about what to do when you're the one growing faster than everyone else, who you go to when you feel afraid of these changes, and how to prepare for your next (or 10th) period.

Sonya does this using language we can all understand, and without judgment or self-doubt.

Sonya has created a movement, not just for any body, but for every body! She's dreaming bigger and doing the work to make sure each one of us understands there is no wrong way to be our full selves in our full bodies. And she has created this book to help you understand the changes in your body and to offer strategies for coping with and loving them. Parents, caretakers, and girls alike will all recognize Sonya's affirming voice as she reminds us that this sometimes confusing—but always exciting—time is yours to enjoy.

—Bianca I. Laureano, MA, CSE
Award-winning reproductive health educator

INTRODUCTION

GUESS WHAT? I AM GOING TO SHARE SOME TOP-SECRET
information with you. Are you ready? Okay here it is . . .
You have a body! And it isn't just any kind of body—it's
an *awesome* body. How do I know this? Because *all*
bodies are awesome and that should never be a secret.
Every girl should shout it from the highest mountaintop:
"Hey world, *my body is awesome*!"

And as the proud owner of an awesome body you
might notice that it is also a changing body. Change
can be wonderful, but it can also be a little confusing at
times. As we get older not only do our bodies change,
but so do our feelings and relationships. With all of
these changes going on, it is only natural to have
some questions. This book is all about helping you get
answers to some of the uncertainties you may have
about wonderfully changing *you*!

If you haven't noticed, I am super excited to be
talking about your body. That might seem a little

weird, but it's because I love helping people understand why they should love their bodies. It started when I was 15 years old and became a peer educator, helping my classmates and other teens learn about how to make good decisions about their bodies. For many years I worked at jobs that were focused on helping people lead healthier lives. A few years ago, I started a company called The Body Is Not An Apology, which is all about how to love our bodies and make a world where everybody has what they need to live their best life. Every day I work to remind people all over the world that every body is magic!

In the years since I started my company, people with all kinds of bodies—from 8 years old to 88 years old—have been part of the workshops I lead about self-love. People with tall bodies, short bodies, wide bodies, slim bodies, bodies with disabilities, bodies of different races—so many cool bodies. Not one of them was the same but each was beautiful and powerful in its own unique way. Today, millions of people have visited the website The Body Is Not An Apology and decided to practice loving their bodies unapologetically. I hope after reading this book you feel ready to do the exact same thing.

Do you know why people are afraid of the dark? Because they can't see what's going on. You should not be in the dark about puberty or the ways your body will change in the coming weeks, months, and years. Knowledge is power and knowing all about the changes in your body will make you an expert on your body. I know you picked up this book to learn about puberty for your-self. But if you read something you don't understand or want to know more about, I strongly encourage you to share those questions with a trusted adult. You are a beautiful, powerful, smart girl who feels confident about her body and her life. Puberty doesn't change that. If anything, puberty is an opportunity to feel even more confident and powerful in your body. Why? Because you are becoming an expert on its awesomeness!

In this book I use the word "girl" to describe the gender of the humans I imagine are reading it. The word "girl" may not feel like the right word to describe you. Maybe you feel more like a boy or maybe you feel like a boy and a girl sometimes. That is okay! You don't have to feel like a girl at all to read this book and learn how your unique body works. The information in these pages will help you understand your body even if the word "girl" isn't the right fit. As you read, you can swap out "girl" for any word that feels good for you and your body. If you have questions about your gender, check out the amazing resources in the back of this book and share them with an adult you trust.

Throughout this book we will discuss some key questions you might have about puberty and body changes. We'll start by discussing what puberty is (the normal body changes that signal your transition into adulthood). Next, we'll talk about some of the body changes you might expect during this time, starting with the small changes (Hey, how did that hair get there?) and then we will move on to discuss the bigger ones like breast development and menstruation. We'll even talk about how you can navigate issues like health, well-being, emotions, and privacy. In each section we'll highlight what physical changes you may notice, as well as share tips about how to care for your body as these changes happen. A glossary in the back of the book will help you understand words that may be new to you.

Puberty is a thrilling time filled with new opportunities to understand your body even better. When we are equipped with correct information, we have everything we need to move into adulthood, certain that our incredible bodies have all they need to help us live an amazing life!

FABULOUS YOU!

. . . .

You are a capable, confident girl. How do I know this? Because you came to the planet that way. All girls—no matter what they look like—are powerful and have all they need to grow into fabulous adults. Puberty may change lots of things about your body, but it should not change your knowing that you are a spectacular human being! Here's what you need to know about puberty.

WHAT IS PUBERTY?

Some adults make puberty seem like a dramatic movie where girls have the starring role. Have you ever seen a film where the mother makes a less-than-nice comment about her daughter's body and the daughter storms out of the room or bursts into tears? High drama! While you may be having some intense moments these days, puberty is definitely not a dramatic film. Puberty is a natural part of having a body. *Everybody* goes through it. You might want to think about it more like an exciting train ride than a high-drama adventure film. If you know where you are headed, puberty can be a wonderful journey and the perfect time to notice and learn about all the brilliant things your body will do on its way to adulthood.

What Does "Puberty" Mean?

Puberty is defined as "the age at or period during which the body of a boy or girl matures and becomes capable of reproducing." Reproducing—having a baby—is a pretty adult thing to do. While puberty doesn't mean you are ready for a baby, it is the time when your body develops and grows in order to one day handle that very adult task. Puberty is the process of your body beginning to move from childhood into adulthood. While that sounds like a big deal—and it is!—there is no need to worry, because puberty doesn't happen overnight. You may already be noticing changes in your body, but puberty is a process that happens over several years. Your body is giving you lots of time to adjust and enjoy the journey.

What to Expect

For most girls, puberty can begin around 8 or 9 years old and usually lasts until they are around 16. Some girls will begin a bit earlier and some girls will start later. Every girl's body is different, and puberty will begin at the time that is right for you.

Puberty comes with lots of changes. Some will be small and easy to get used to, while other changes will feel enormous. Just remember that your body is really smart; it knows exactly what it needs to do to help you grow into an adult. Here are some of the changes you can expect to see during puberty:

Nature's Chemicals

Once you start puberty, your body will begin to release new hormones—chemicals that help kick off all the changes you will experience during this time.

Everything's Growing

One of the first changes you may notice is your body beginning to grow, sometimes much faster than you're used to. You may start getting taller, curvier, or rounder (specifically around the hips and legs). It all depends on your individual body.

Breast Development

One of the major changes during puberty is the development of breasts. How fast your breasts grow and how big they will become is another part of your journey that will be unique. Breasts come in all sorts of shapes and sizes. Often, one breast will grow faster than the other. Your breasts may grow big or they may grow small; either way is just fine. There is no breast size that is better than another. Whether your breasts grow very quickly or seem like they are taking their own sweet time, remember that their timing will be perfect for your body!

Hair Down Where?

You may notice you are sprouting hair in all sorts of new places, including under your arms and on your vulva and

pubic mound (the space right below your belly). The hair that grows on your genitals or private areas is called pubic hair. If you find the hair on your arms or legs is growing thicker and darker, no worries. That is also part of the puberty ride.

Let It Flow

During puberty your body will begin to produce new fluids. This may mean your skin will get a bit oilier (this is often the main cause of acne) and you may find that you sweat a bit more than you used to. We will talk about ways to stay feeling fresh and clean during puberty a little later on, but know that all of these changes are exactly what most girls go through on the puberty train.

Perhaps one of the biggest parts of puberty is the start of menstruation (getting your period). In many cultures, getting your period is a very special and important time in a girl's life. For others, it's just another interesting thing the body does. For some girls, their first period will be a few light drops of blood in their underwear. However, if you have a heavier period, that is okay, too. The blood can be bright or dark red, or even more of a brownish color. Since everyone's body is different, there is no one way to have a period.

Before or between your periods you may also notice a clear or white fluid in your underpants. This is called discharge and it is totally normal. We will talk about it more in the chapters ahead.

Feeling All the Feelings

While there are lots of things happening on the outside of your body during puberty, there are also plenty of things happening inside that will bring about some interesting changes. One of those changes has to do with your emotions. The hormones that your body produces during this time may intensify your emotions at a time when you may also be receiving more responsibilities or pressures because you are getting older. All of these new experiences in your body and in your world can make for an emotional time. Anger, sadness, frustration, and tiredness are all feelings you might have, sometimes all in the same day. Be kind and patient with yourself. Your body is going through an extraordinary transition, so give yourself a big heap of extra love.

What Is Normal?

One of the most common questions girls ask about all the changes happening during puberty is, "Hey, is this normal?" Here is the short answer to that question: Yes! Your body will experience all sorts of new sensations and functions during this important time in your life. Growing very quickly or watching your body change shape may feel unusual. You may not even enjoy some of the changes that come with puberty. This is all okay.

While the changes that are happening in your body are similar to the changes happening in the bodies of other girls your age, your body is special because it is all yours. This means that your puberty experience will be your own sort of normal. In fact, being different *is* normal! The more you trust and listen to your body, the easier it will be to tell if something is going on that needs special attention. For example, if something in your body feels painful or uncomfortable during this time, you should talk to a trusted adult about it right away.

Every Body Is a Great Body

Artist Glenn Marla says, "There is no wrong way to have a body!" and no truer words have ever been spoken. No matter how your body changes during puberty, always remember that your body is a gift and it will always be one of a kind.

Of course, you won't always feel that your body is a gift. In fact, there will be times you might ask yourself some pretty tough questions like:

"Is my body still amazing even if I am two feet taller than the tallest boy in the class?"

"Why am I the heaviest person in my class?"

"Why don't I want to dress like the other girls? I'd rather wear baseball caps and play sports."

"Why do I feel strange and weird and different?"

No matter how out of place you might feel during this time, there is one thing that remains true: *you* have an absolutely *incredible* body! No one else can be you, and it is your *youness* that makes you so special. Girls come in all shapes, sizes, colors, and abilities—and no one type is better than another.

GROWING AND CHANGING

So far, there has been only one other time in your whole life where your body changed as much as it is changing now . . . and you were still eating baby food when that happened. While puberty does not make you an adult, it is a new stage in your growth, and there are all sorts

of new information you will need in order to take care of your developing body. The puberty train is preparing to pull into the first station.

First Signs of Puberty

You may be asking yourself, "How in the world will I know that I have started puberty?" The answer is this: All you have to do is listen to your body—it will start dropping some hints that your journey has begun.

But before you even begin to see the changes happening to your body, many of those changes will have already begun *inside* you. Your ovaries, which are parts of your body that produce hormones, will begin signaling that it's time for all the other changes to start. It is during this time that you may grow taller or curvier than you were before. This sudden burst of bigger is called a growth spurt, and we will talk more about it in chapter 2.

Up Next . . . Breasts

Remember those hormones that started signaling the rest of your body to board the puberty train? Well, they have also sent a message to your breasts to begin growing. The first thing you may notice is some soreness or tenderness and a hard bump just underneath your nipple. The bump may make the dark circles around your nipples (called your areola) look bigger or puffy. The hard bump is called a breast bud and it is the first sign of budding breasts.

Pubic Hair

Some girls will begin to see signs of pubic hair before they begin growing breasts. Remember, each girl's body is different, and your body will do whatever is perfect for you. You may first see fine thin hairs under your armpits and in your pubic area. That hair will eventually grow darker, thicker, and sometimes curly. In chapter 4, we will talk all about the best ways to care for the hair down there.

Period Please

Usually, once you have begun to develop breasts and pubic hair, it is a sign that you may soon get your period. Some girls get their period at younger ages, like 9 or 10 years old. Other girls may start when they are older, sometimes as old as 15 or 16. There may be lots of chatter at school among the girls about who got their period first. But ovaries can't race and getting your period is not a competition. Whenever your period starts, it will be the right time for you.

More Hair

There are lots of hair happenings during puberty, and soon you will go from light wisps of hair to thicker, darker hair on your arms, legs, and pubic area. Hair can begin sprouting as early as 8 or 9, but it can also wait until your period begins to show up. You may hear other girls talk about shaving. Shaving is a personal choice that is all about what you want to do with your body. We'll talk more about that a little later, in chapter 2.

Puberty Timeline

If you are sitting at home counting the hours until puberty arrives, you may be waiting awhile because puberty has its own schedule. You can, however, look at a general timeline of when these body changes usually begin. Below is the puberty train schedule. Just remember, this train does its own thing. It may show up early and it often shows up late. Either way, you will get through puberty right on time.

7-11: Your body begins making hormones, which signal to the rest of your body that puberty is ready to start.

9-14: You develop breast buds and your breasts begin to grow.

9-15: You may get your first period. This usually happens one or two years after you begin breast development. Many girls get their period between 12 and 13, but some girls start as early as 9 or as late as 15. If you haven't had a period by 16, you should talk to a trusted adult about getting a checkup.

10-16: Pubic hair may begin to be visible. Some girls may notice hair as early as 7 or 8. During this time, hair under the armpits and on the legs may grow darker and thicker.

15-16: By this time puberty is usually in full swing. You may be approaching the height you will be as an adult, and your breasts may be done growing, too. If your period is regular, it will begin showing up about once a month. Many girls do not have regular periods at this age. We'll talk more about this later.

Remember that puberty is stubborn, not arriving even one second before it's ready. And that's fine—just enjoy your body exactly as it is today. Tomorrow you can enjoy your body however it is then!

The Rate of Change

You may have questions like, "How much hair am I going to get?" or "Will I get giant breasts or tiny breasts?" Unfortunately, there is no way of knowing. Your body has its own recipe for puberty. How fast these changes will happen—and what your body will look like when you are all finished—is something only your body knows. Right now, all you need to know is that your body is working with you to help you grow into a powerful young person. You are starting out with a body you love and you absolutely can finish puberty with a body you love—and maybe you'll love it even more!

YOUR CHANGING BODY

. . . .

Now that you know a little more about what puberty is and what you can expect to see along the journey, let's dig into the specifics about the changes you may experience during this wild and wonderful time. The most valuable thing you can carry into puberty is confidence and power. Your body is perfect exactly as it is today, and it will be perfect during and after puberty, no matter how it changes! Let's explore all the fascinating details of these exciting changes.

HEIGHT AND WEIGHT

At the end of the last chapter you discovered that there is no way of knowing what your body will look like after you go through puberty because only your body knows. How is it that your body has all this secret information? One word: Genes.

All humans are born with genes and they hold the key to what sort of body you have now and what sort of body you will have after you go through puberty. Genes decide whether you will be short or tall, heavier or lighter, whether your eyes are an enchanting brown or a mesmerizing green. Every human on the planet has a set of genes and each set of genes is different.

While everyone has their own set, sometimes we will have genes that are like our family's genes. Knowing this can give us a small clue as to what our bodies may look like after puberty. If most of the women in your family are shorter, chances are good that you will be shorter. This is true of hair color, breast size, and weight.

But there is no 100 percent guarantee that your body will look like your family members' bodies. Your genes have their own top-secret recipe that will make your body one of a kind.

Growth Spurts

Puberty means your body is going to get bigger and stronger. It also means you can expect to grow out of your clothes much faster than usual. This season of rapid growth is called a growth spurt. During a growth spurt your arms, legs, feet, and hands all get bigger. For a short period of time you may feel a bit like a baby giraffe learning how to move around with new longer limbs. Baby giraffes are adorable, and just like them, you will soon start to feel at home in your changing body.

How Fast and How High

Your growth will continue over the next four to eight years, and other parts of puberty will happen between these spurt seasons. For instance, around 85 percent of girls will develop breast buds after their first growth spurt. Pubic hair and acne usually follow next. Not too long after these changes, you are likely to have another growth spurt, which is often one of the biggest of your growing years. In fact, most girls can expect to grow anywhere from two to three inches in just a few months during this time. Usually there is one more big growth spurt that occurs after your period has begun. Girls often grow an additional one to two inches around this time, but it is not uncommon to grow as much as three additional inches.

Ouch! Will It Hurt?

Don't worry, your body is ready for this ride. During this time of extra growth, some girls experience what we call "growing pains." Growing pains are not actually a result of your body growing (most of your bone growth happens while you are sleeping), but are common aches and pains in your muscles that come and go. Doctors are not sure what causes these growing pains, but doing exercises like stretches before bed can help you navigate some of the discomfort.

★ ★ GET SOME CALCIUM ★ ★

During any growth spurt, it is especially important to make sure your bones are healthy and strong. One of the best ways to care for your growing bones is to be certain you are getting enough calcium in your diet. Calcium is the mineral that gives your bones strength, and without it you can develop some serious bone diseases later in life. Doctors say girls between the ages of 9 and 18 should have about four servings of high-calcium foods and drinks per day to give their bones what they need to stay strong. Milk happens to be high in calcium and is a simple way to get calcium nutrients to your growing bones, but it is not the only way to stock up. Leafy green veggies like kale and broccoli, yogurt, and sardines are all high in calcium, too.

Getting enough sleep, exercise, and good food will also go a long way toward easing many of the uncomfortable side effects of puberty, including growing pains. We will talk more about some healthy habits later. For now, just know that growing pains are a regular part of having a growing body. However, talk to an adult if you feel serious pain in your joints (your knees, ankles, or elbows).

Ask an Adult: Scoliosis

As you go through puberty there will be lots of new things you will notice about your body. Most of them will be typical changes most girls go through while moving into the teenage years. But occasionally your body might be alerting you to a more serious issue. In those cases, you should always tell a trusted adult what's going on.

Some young people discover that, as their bodies begin to grow quickly, their spines stop growing straight and begin to curve like the letter S. This curve in the spine is called scoliosis. Sometimes scoliosis is easy to notice because it may look like you are leaning to one side or one of your shoulders is higher than the other. The school nurse or your pediatrician may give you an exam to check your spine. Most scoliosis is minimal and doesn't require any treatment, but some might need more help. To learn more about scoliosis you should talk to your school nurse, doctor, or another trusted adult.

Shape and Weight Changes

Shape and weight changes are just another stop on the puberty train. One thing you should absolutely remember during this time is that your body knows what size and shape it is supposed to be, and if you take good care of your body you will help it become the best body it can be for you.

Girls get lots of messages about their bodies and what they "should" look like. Well, those messages are silly because we each have our own unique body that doesn't need to look like anybody else's. Earlier in this chapter we talked about how your genes determine much about how your body will look after puberty. Genes also determine what shape your body will have. Maybe you will be short and lean like your aunt, or perhaps you will be tall and round like your grandma. Your genes hold all your top-secret body information, which also means that you can be as tall and weigh just as much as someone else and still have bodies that look completely different.

During puberty you may notice that your body is getting softer and rounder around the hips and thighs.

You may also see that your waist is getting narrower and that there is more fat around your upper arms and back. These changes in your weight and shape usually follow the same timeline as your height changes. As you get taller you will also get heavier. Part of your weight gain will also involve your breasts getting bigger. The best way to stay healthy and strong during this part of puberty is to eat lots of healthy fresh foods and to move your body in ways that are fun and make you feel good and fit.

Fat's Where It's At!

There are people who use the word *fat* to make fun of people or be mean. Someone obviously forgot to tell them that all bodies are good bodies.

Fat gets a bad reputation, which is terrible because everybody needs fat. Growing a healthy body during puberty means you need to grow muscle *and* body fat. Some bodies are naturally heavier than other bodies, and your body needs to have some fat on it to get through puberty.

Why is fat so important? Well, it helps your brain think, your inside organs work, your hair grow, your eyes see, and so much more. Without fat your body would simply not have the energy to get through puberty. And losing too much fat on our bodies can cause all kinds of problems like weak bones, damaged and dull hair, and even organ failure. Let's stop giving fat a bad rap!

★ ★ DIET? DON'T! ★ ★

Diets are bad news, and yet we still see commercials for them every day on television and in magazines. You might be wondering, if diets aren't good for us, why do people keep telling us to go on them? The short answer is money. People who make commercials and sell diets make lots of money by convincing people to buy their products even when they don't need them.

Diets are especially bad for young girls because they can keep your body from getting the necessary nutrition it needs to be able to get through puberty. If you are worried about whether your body is healthy, talk to your school nurse or doctor. They can check things like your heart, lungs, blood pressure, and other signs related to your health. There are also websites about being healthy at every size. I've listed some at the back of this book.

Embrace Your Body

Just like there are television commercials and magazine ads that try to tell girls that fat is bad, there are also messages that tell girls that they must have big breasts and curves to be real girls. Of course, you know that is ridiculous because there is no such thing as a "real" girl. If you feel like a girl, you *are* a girl! Your genes, which are specially made only for you, may mean you are going to be tall and thin or short and thin. Being a girl with a thin body is just as good as being a girl with a curvy or round body. There is no such thing as a better body than any other. No matter what, your body is growing into the body it was meant to be—perfect for you!

YOUR CHANGING HAIR AND SKIN

Just as your body is changing its shape and size, other parts of you are changing, too. Here are some more changes you may notice.

Hair, There, and Everywhere

Your hair growth and color are determined by your genes. (Genes are bossy little things, aren't they?) This means you get to spend less time worrying about what you will look like and more time thinking about the great ways you can take care of the fabulous hair and skin your genes gave you.

Your Head of Hair

Don't believe the commercials that show women swinging around their long, flowing, bouncy hair. That is not what most girls' hair looks like. Hair, like girls, comes in all varieties: short, long, fine, coarse,

curly, kinky, straight, wavy, brown, red, black, blond, chestnut, auburn, mahogany, golden, strawberry . . . the possibilities are nearly endless.

Just as there are lots of different kinds of hair, there are many ways to care for your specific hair type. For instance, if you have straight fine hair that gets oily quickly, you may need to wash your hair more often, like every other day. If you are a girl with curlier, kinkier hair that tends to be drier, washing your hair that often may cause dandruff (flakes of dead skin from your scalp) or hair breakage. In that case, washing your hair once a week might work better for you.

No matter what kind of hair you have, you will want to make sure that it is clean and brushed and combed daily. To find a shampoo and conditioner you like, you may need to try a few, but there is no reason to spend tons of money. Expensive does not necessarily mean better. There are tons of great natural hair care videos on YouTube that will help you find the best hair care process for you. (Check out the links at the back of this book.)

Fur Fever

For many girls, the first sign of puberty they notice is the development of breast buds, but for about 15 percent of girls the first sign of puberty is pubic hair. Almost everyone gets some hair, but how much you will get and where will vary. Our pubic hair usually matches the other hair already on our bodies. That means if you have lighter hair on your head you are likely to have lighter body hair. If you have darker hair you may notice darker hair growing on your body. Your hair may be thick, thin, fine, or coarse, all depending on . . . you guessed it, your genes.

But Where?

You may first notice hair under your arms and between your legs on your pubic mound (the soft skin just below your belly). Fine hair may also appear on your arms and legs, and occasionally girls get a few hairs on their breasts. Girls sometimes even get hair on their upper lips, backs, and chins. Yes, hair just about anywhere is normal. After all, humans are mammals and all mammals have hair.

To Shave or Not to Shave?

You may have already heard lots of people talking about shaving the hair on their bodies. Whether you choose to shave is a personal choice only you can make. No matter what you decide, you should remember that having hair on your body is a natural part of puberty and you absolutely do not have to get rid of it if you don't want to. Shaving is sort of like diets: Companies make tons of money trying to convince you to buy their hair removal products. They want you to start shaving now so that you will buy shaving cream and razors forever.

Keep in mind, though, that some people choose to shave under their arms to keep body odor at bay. During puberty the new hormones in your body may cause you to sweat more. Sweat by itself does not have an odor, but when it mixes with tiny bacteria trapped in the hairs under your arms or between your legs, it can get a bit smelly. Shaving is not the only way to deal with body odor, and we will talk about some other options to manage body smells a little later. If you do decide to shave under your arms, talk to a trusted adult who can help you find a good razor and a moisturizing shaving cream. You want to be sure you have a new razor to avoid getting little bumps or a rash in the spot where you shaved. And don't forget, when you shave, the area is often itchy while the hair grows back.

The Skin You Are In

Did you know that your skin is the biggest organ of your entire body? From head to toe that is some serious ground to cover. And while your skin will need some extra attention during puberty to keep you glowing, don't worry. The key to healthy skin is simple: give it water, rest, and good food.

Pimples and Blackheads

One of the concerns girls often have during puberty is whether they will get acne (also known as pimples). What you should know is that puberty does not have to doom you to a life of acne cream and zits. While you may get some acne during this time, having a good skin care routine can help keep breakouts to a minimum. But pimples are indeed another part of puberty that many of us have to go through. When your body begins producing the hormones that signal puberty to start, you also begin producing extra oil inside your body. That excess oil often mixes with sweat and dirt and can clog your pores (small openings on your skin). Those clogged pores cause acne and blackheads.

Washing your face daily with a gentle cleanser and following up with a moisturizer should help clear away much of the bacteria that causes acne. If you find that you are having a more severe breakout, you may want to go the drugstore with a trusted adult and purchase some anti-acne cream with a bit of medicine in it. Be

sure to look for something that is oil- and soap-free, since it is better for your skin.

Sometimes skin breakouts can become more serious than drugstore treatments can manage. If you are experiencing difficult acne that won't go away, ask an adult to take you to see a dermatologist (skin doctor). He or she can give you stronger medicine to help with breakouts.

Sun Fun

Everyone's skin needs sun, but how much really depends on what kind of skin you have. The sun's rays can feel great on our bodies, but too much sun can be

Pimples are a common part of growing up. They are so common that 85 percent of teenagers will have acne during their teen years. That means almost everybody has pimples.

dangerous for some skin types. If you have lighter or paler skin, you should always wear sunscreen because sunlight can penetrate your skin more easily and cause sunburn. Spending too much time out in the sun without sunscreen can also cause serious diseases like skin cancer, no matter what color your skin is.

Look for a sunscreen with a 30+ SPF (sun protection factor) and make sure it's waterproof. Even if you are not swimming you may still be sweating, and you don't want the sunscreen to run off.

If you have darker skin, this means it is harder for the sun's rays to penetrate your skin. While this may mean you are less likely to get sunburn, it also means that some of the nutrients we get from the sun—particularly vitamin D—will be a bit more difficult for you to soak up. Because of this, you may need to try to get sun more often. Even if you don't have darker skin but wear a headscarf or covering as part of your religion or culture, look for opportunities to give your body a little sun when you can. It will thank you later!

Shades of You

Girls come in all different shades and colors. You may be pale pink, deep dark brown, or hundreds of shades in between. The difference in human skin colors all depends on where your ancestors are from. If your great-great-great-great-great-great grandparents were from colder places like Europe, you will likely have paler, lighter skin. If your ancestors were from warmer places like Africa, the Middle East, or island nations like Samoa or Puerto Rico, you will likely have medium to darker brown skin.

Some people spend lots of money and time trying to change the color of their skin. Some girls spend hours in the sun or at salons trying to get a tan while other girls buy bleaching cream and other products to try to make their skin lighter. Constant tanning or skin lightening is harmful to your skin. Not to mention that the color of your skin is *fabulous* just as it is!

Bumps, Blisters, and Warts . . . Okay

During puberty our bodies do all sorts of new and unusual things that may surprise you or seem a bit weird. One of those things involves viruses that have been asleep in our bodies, which then wake up and begin showing signs and symptoms. It's all part of the puberty ride. You may notice bumps where there were never bumps before, sometimes on your arms or legs. These bumps may be warts caused by a virus called human papillomavirus (HPV). Because HPV is transmitted by skin-to-skin contact, the virus already lives in some bodies but may not show signs until later, in the form of small bumps. If you notice warts on your body, don't pick, scratch, or rub them, as it can make them spread. Talk with an adult about getting some medicine at the drugstore that can help them go away. If you notice warts in your genital area, ask a trusted adult to take you to see a doctor who can tell you the best way to treat them.

Another sneaky virus that is sometimes hanging out quietly in our bodies is called herpes simplex virus (HSV-1). This virus can cause cold sores, which are uncomfortable blisters on or around the mouth and lips. Cold sores are also contagious, so don't touch or pick at it if you have one. You may get cold sores on and off over the years because the virus will always live in your body. You can avoid contracting the virus or having frequent flare-ups by not sharing things like lipstick or lip balm, toothbrushes, or drinks with someone with a cold sore. You should also stay away from too much sun, stress, or acidic foods like oranges and lemons as they affect how often and how uncomfortable cold sores can be. If you get a cold sore, you can find treatments at the drugstore to put on your lips that will help the sore heal more quickly. If you are getting cold sores often or they are painful, talk to an adult about seeing a doctor. He or she may be able to prescribe medicine to help.

Smell Me

One day you may come home after running around playing and find yourself saying, "What is that smell?" only to realize it's you. You have just discovered you are developing body odor. Remember that your body is producing increased hormones and there are new sweat glands under your arms, feet, and between your legs. This combination can sometimes be a little smelly. But body odor is a common part of puberty, and with good hygiene practices you can come out smelling like a rose!

You sweat and create bacteria every single day, so you will need to wash your body daily. Pay special attention to your underarms, feet, and genitals. You can buy different types of deodorant or antiperspirant to counter body odor under your arms. Deodorants will not keep you from sweating, but they will keep the sweat from being stinky. Be sure not to use too much, as many people can be sensitive to the chemicals in deodorant. Antiperspirants keep your body from producing sweat. You should only use antiperspirants under your arms. Sweat is a necessary function of your body and without it you can become overheated or even get sick.

BODY BASICS

As your body grows and changes, you will need to focus on taking good care of it along the way. Taking care of your body is one of the best ways to show that you love it. Here are some basics that will help you be a good buddy to your great body.

Smile for a Mile

Growing up means losing those baby teeth and moving in some massive molars. Okay, maybe not massive, but it is true that the teeth you get when your baby teeth fall out are the teeth you will have for the rest of your life. There is no better time than the present to take care of them.

To keep your teeth healthy and strong you should brush at least twice daily and floss after every meal. When you don't keep up with your brushing and flossing you can develop plaque and tartar on your teeth. Plaque is the gritty film you feel on your teeth when you haven't brushed for a while, and is made of bacteria that hide out in your mouth waiting to grow. Left for too long, the bacteria will cause bad breath and other problems, like tartar. Tartar is hardened plaque buildup that has been on your teeth awhile. It can cause yellowing of the teeth and tooth decay.

Be sure to brush for at least two full minutes to ensure you are getting rid of plaque and avoiding tartar buildup. You can also keep your teeth strong by avoiding sugary foods and beverages like soft drinks, juices, and candy. They are cavity and tooth-decay culprits.

Make sure an adult takes you to see a dentist at least once a year for a professional dental cleaning and to help determine if you need braces or other medical dental care. The good dental habits you develop now will last you a lifetime (and will help your teeth last that long, too!).

Braces

As you move into puberty, you may find that you will need braces if your teeth are not coming in straight or if you have an overbite or underbite. Braces have come a long way. Today, braces can be metal, invisible, ceramic, or only worn at bedtime, and some even come with little rubber bands in cool colors you can pick out yourself. Braces can be fun. Your dentist will recommend you visit an orthodontist if it looks like you need braces.

Ear, Eye, and Nail Care

Along with your teeth, other parts of your body require a little more care once you've entered puberty.

Piercings

Do you love earrings? Perhaps your ears are already pierced, or you are thinking about getting a cool new piercing just like your best friend, but either way, piercing your ears or any other part of your body is a big deal. Piercings can look cool, but they can also cause dangerous infections if they are not done properly. It is very important that you only allow a professional to pierce your body. You should also make sure that the professional piercer uses a brand-new needle every time, equipment that has *never* been used on anyone else before, and that everything is sterilized.

While getting your earlobes pierced doesn't generally hurt much and heals pretty quickly, this is not true for all piercing sites on your body. Some parts of your body can take a very long time to heal or may be more prone to infection than others. Talk with an adult before you do any piercing. You should know that it is against the law to pierce anyone under 16 or 18 (depending on where you live) without a parent's permission.

Jeepers Peepers, Look at Those Eyes

Whether mahogany brown, aqua green, or bluish with specks of orange that glitter in the sun, your eyes need your care and attention. Eye shadow and mascara can be fun to play around with, but they can damage your eyes if you are not careful. If you wear eye makeup, be sure to use a gentle eye-makeup remover and wash your face with warm water before bed each night. Sleeping in your makeup is not good for your skin and absolutely not healthy for your eyes.

Don't forget that just like everything else, your eyeballs are growing during puberty, too! This rapid eye growth can cause vision issues like myopia (also known as nearsightedness). Myopia means you can see things when they are up close but may have trouble seeing them when they are far away. If you notice that images in the distance are fuzzy, you must squint to see things, or you are getting headaches often, these may be signs that you are nearsighted. You should tell an adult and have an eye doctor check out your eyes.

Myopia is treated by getting prescription glasses or contact lenses. Because of your age, you will likely get glasses. Glasses can be a fabulous fashion statement, so get creative! You can get a pair with polka dots or

stripes. You can have hot pink frames or play it safe with black frames. Whatever you choose, glasses are a great way to express all the fun and fascinating things about you!

Twinkle Toes, Hot Hands, and Nailing Down Care

On the puberty train it can be easy to miss the hands, feet, and nails stop, especially with all the other exciting sights to see. But these parts of your body need your attention because their care is necessary for a healthy, happy body. Keeping your hands clean can reduce the germs and bacteria that get transmitted to your face and cause acne breakouts, colds, and other infections. Every time you go to the bathroom you should wash your hands thoroughly. A good hand washing that kills those nasty germs should take about 20 seconds. (Here's a helpful tip: singing the alphabet song all the way through at a normal pace takes about 23 seconds.)

Because you are producing new sweat glands during puberty you may also notice that your feet have become a bit sweaty. Sweaty feet can equal smelly feet. The best way to avoid smelliness is to wash, wash, wash. Be sure to change your socks daily and keep your feet dry and moisturized—this will help keep down the stinky smells.

Nails can be a spectacular way to express yourself and your personality, but to do so you will need to practice some nail care. Nail biting is a no-no, as it can cause hangnails (soreness and broken skin around the nail bed), which makes it easier to get infections. Biting your nails also means all the dirt underneath your nail is now in your mouth . . . yuck. Ask an older sibling or an adult to show you how to use a nail clipper to cut your nails and file them, which will help them grow stronger. Filing your nails evenly across instead of pointed will also prevent them from breaking as often.

Manicures and pedicures are lovely, and picking cool colors can be another way to show off your personality, but you should be careful. Artificial nails can weaken your natural nails and damage them over time. It is also possible that you may be allergic to the chemicals in nail polishes and remover. Much like piercings, you want to be certain that the person giving you a manicure or pedicure only uses tools that have been sterilized before they use them on you. Doing your own manicures and pedicures at home can be lots of fun and save some precious pennies.

BREASTS
AND BRAS

· ·

We have arrived at one of the busiest stations on
the puberty train, breast central. Pulling into this
station will usually happen over several years with
lots of short stops along the way. No matter when
you arrive, breast development is a major body
change during puberty that you will want to feel
ready for. Together we will make sure you have all
you need to know to feel confident and powerful
as you learn how to care for your growing and
changing body.

A NEW SHAPE: DEVELOPING BREASTS

Over the last 8 to 11 years you have probably gotten pretty used to your body and the unique way it looks. It's kind of like a sweater that you have had for a while, comfortable and familiar. Sure, your body has gotten taller. Your feet have gotten bigger. But for the most part, you have known your body for a while, and it can be a big adjustment to make when your body begins to look very different and change in ways that sometimes feel like they happened overnight. Before you wake up wondering, "Hey, when did my flat chest become a landscape of rolling hills?", let's talk about exactly what you can expect when you start developing breasts.

Breast development is one of the body changes that puts puberty front and center, but it doesn't all happen overnight. There are actually five stages of breast development and they occur over several years. Whether you are about to dive into stage 1 or are swimming in stage 3, here's what you should know about your breasts as they grow and change.

What's Already There

These are the stages of breast development that you will encounter:

Stage 1 Preadolescent Breasts
Around 8 to 11 years old

Before we start talking about how breasts grow, we should begin where we all begin. You already have nipples. Nipples are the small buttons of skin on top of your areolae, those darker circles on your chest. Your nipples may be flat or pointy. Sometimes they start off flat but become erect when it's cold outside—they are sensitive little things! Nipples have tiny holes in them you cannot see, and those itty-bitty holes will one day release the milk humans make to feed new babies. Yes, just like cows, humans make milk, too! In fact, all mammals make milk.

Stage 2 Breast Buds
Around 10 to 11½ years old

If you remember from chapter 1, the first thing you may notice as you begin breast development is a hard, nickel-size lump just underneath your nipple called a breast bud. Breast buds form when the breast tissue and milk glands begin to grow. Breast buds can be so small that you might not even notice they are there. But they can make your breast area sore and tender.

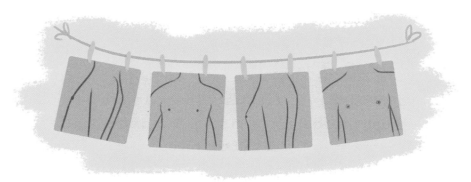

If you feel some slight discomfort, don't worry. It is just your breasts doing exactly what they are supposed to do. You may have breast buds that are completely different sizes, or you may have a bud in one breast but not in the other. How your breasts will grow cannot be compared with any of your friends'. Your experience will be all your own, so don't let anyone tell you how your breasts "should" look. Breast development is different for every girl. Your body knows what it is doing, even when that looks different from what other people's bodies are doing.

Stage 3 Breast Growth
Around 11½ to 13 years old

After you have developed breast buds your breasts will begin to grow more fatty tissue and milk glands. At this stage you may notice that your breasts are slightly cone shaped. During this time, you may also notice that your areolae are getting bigger and puffier. These signs mean your puberty train is on the right track.

Stage 4 Onset of Puberty
Around 13 to 15 years old

During this stage your breasts will begin to lose the cone shape they developed in stage 3 and start to take on the size and shape of the breasts you will have in adulthood. The changes to your breast shape in this stage are mostly caused by a hormone called estrogen. Estrogen is sort of the body's puberty boss, telling it when it is time to go to work and when the job is done. Estrogen bosses around lots of other parts of puberty besides your breasts and is also in control of menstruation. Most girls will get their first period during stage 4 or 5 of breast development. We'll talk more about that soon. For now, just know that when you arrive at this stage you are usually in full-on puberty.

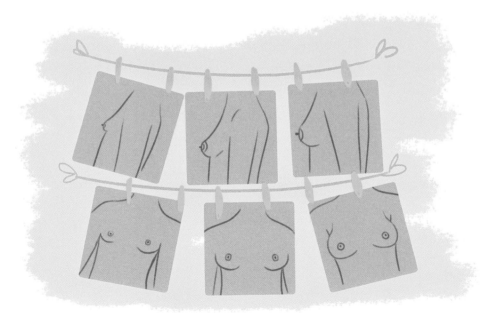

Stage 5 Mature Breasts
Around 15 and older

Stage 5 is the final stage of puberty breast development. At this stage your breasts have reached maturity and are the size and shape they will likely be in adulthood. The average girl will take three to five years to go from the first stage to the fifth stage of breast development, but for some girls it can take up to 10 years. Remember, this is a major stop on a long ride!

Your Timeline Is Just Fine

Right now, you may be saying, "But I'm already 10 and I'm not in stage 2, what's up with that?" Or you might be saying, "What a minute! I'm 9 and I'm already in stage 3. What's going on with me?" What is going on is that only your body and its secret puberty recipe knows when you will go through each stage and how quickly. It is important to be patient with your body as it changes.

It is also important to notice the changes that are happening, as sometimes there might be things going on that only an adult can help with. For instance, some girls start puberty before their body is totally ready for it. This is called precocious puberty. Other girls may start much later, which is called delayed puberty. If you are noticing puberty changes starting in your body and you are under 8 years old, or if you are 14 or older and have not noticed any changes yet, talk with a trusted adult who can have a doctor check you out and make sure your puberty train is on the right schedule.

Fifty percent of women have one breast that is smaller than the other. The left one is usually the smaller one and doctors are not sure why.

Shapes and Sizes and All Sorts of Surprises

You might notice that people talk about breasts a lot in commercials, movies, and television shows. Here's the deal: breasts are amazing. After all, your body grows a whole new organ so that one day, if you want, you can feed a baby from your body. That is pretty impressive! Breasts are awesome because of what they can do, not how they look. Big breasts are not better than small breasts and small breasts are not better than big breasts.

If we travel back in time to chapter 1, you will remember that we talked about how our genes decide most of what our bodies will look like after puberty. Genes also determine the size and shape of our breasts. Your breasts may be the size of kiwi fruit or tangerines. They might be grapefruit size or smaller, like plums. There are as many breast shapes and sizes as there are girls on the planet. Whatever shape your breasts are is the right shape and size for your body.

GETTING A BRA: DO I NEED ONE?

Whether getting your first bra is cause for a party or something you're dreading, it should be comfortable on your body and feel like an expression of you. The first thing you should know is every girl does not have to wear a bra, and many girls and women don't. Bras are designed to help make movement a little easier when you are running, jumping, dancing, playing sports, or doing other bouncy activities. This means you don't really need a bra until your breasts are big enough that you feel them moving around under your clothes, or if they are sore and tender and you want some extra cushion between your breasts and your tops.

If wearing a bra doesn't feel helpful or comfortable for you, that is totally okay! Sometimes we feel pressure to wear a bra because we see them on television or because our friends are wearing them already. Anytime you feel pressured into doing something, it is a good sign that it is probably not a great idea to do it.

But if you feel you are ready for a bra you should talk to an adult about it.

Finding the Right Size and Style for You

There are 100 billion different kinds of bras. Okay, maybe that's an exaggeration, but there *are* a lot and sorting through them all can be a bit overwhelming.

♥ YOU HAVE COMPANY! ♥

Millions of women have had the experience of growing breasts and getting their first bra. For some girls it can be a special time. For others, it is not a big deal or may even be a little annoying. All of these reactions are perfectly okay. Here are the reactions of a few women who came before you:

"I don't remember shopping for my first bra, but I remember that all day long the first day I wore it I kept pulling down the neck of my shirt to show my BFF the little rose that was stitched in the front."

-TIGRESS O.

. . . .

"I begged for a bra. Begged. I thought what they represented was so cool. Finally, in the fifth grade my mom said it was time. My mom helped me pick out two or three bras and matching underwear and we had lunch at a Mexican restaurant . . . My mom was great at making something regular so special."

-NICOLE H.

. . . .

"I was in fourth grade and did not want to be a girl . . . I was also the only girl of color and was developing bigger faster. In fifth grade I took my dad's Ace bandages and tried to flatten [my breasts]. My mom took me to the department store and let me pick out what I wanted. I bought all sports bras until high school."

-AYANNA G.

Luckily, when you are just beginning puberty the choices are pretty simple. Many girls at the beginning of breast development start off with a training bra. Training bras are generally made of soft stretchy cotton material without the underwire or padding in bras that are made for bigger breasts. Training bras may even look like a crop top or half tank top. You may also want to check out sports bras, which are designed in a similar way to training bras but are often tighter. This is because they are designed to hold your breasts down when you're playing sports or running. You do not have to be playing sports to wear them, though. They make good first bras if you want something that is a bit simpler in style.

Figuring Out Your Size

If you are in stage 3 and your breasts are starting to be visible through your clothes, you may want to consider a soft cup bra. The best way to know if you are ready for a soft cup bra is to get measured. Your measurements will help you figure out what size bra you will need. In the United States, bras are determined by two measurements: your chest size and your cup size. You can get yourself measured by a professional in the bra department at most retail stores, or you can figure out your chest size on your own.

Simply run a tape measure around your back and under your breasts. If you add five to the number of inches you measured, that number will be your chest size. To figure out your cup size, run the tape measure around your back again, but this time run it across the fullest part of your breasts. Subtract your chest measurement from that figure. What's left should be a number between 1 inch and 4 inches and this will determine your cup. Here's how those sizes work out:

Less than 1 inch = AA

1 inch = A

2 inches = B

3 inches = C

4 inches = D

If your measurement falls somewhere in between, you should round up. It is better to grow into your right size than to start off in a size too small, especially since your body is growing quickly. If you are an A cup or higher it may be time for a soft cup bra.

Some bras are made with underwire. Underwire can be helpful if you have large breasts and need some extra support, but they are not very helpful when you are just starting off. For now, stick to elastic bands and avoid the underwires.

When you get your bra, you may want to match it with your skin color, which will make it less visible under your clothes. If you have dark skin, a dark bra will not be as visible as a white or light-colored bra under a white shirt. If you have lighter skin, you will want a lighter colored bra that is closer to your skin color.

How Does This Thing Work?

Hooks and straps and cups, oh my! Figuring out how to put on a bra can seem a little complicated. None of us were born with this particular skill set, so don't be afraid to ask your mom, big sister, or another trusted adult to help you out.

For the most part, there are two ways people put on bras. The first is to lean forward and slip your arms through the straps, letting your breasts fall into the cups. Once you stand up straight you can reach around and fasten the hooks in the back. You want to make sure that the back band of the bra sits just below your shoulder blades. (Some bras hook in the front, which makes the whole process easier.)

The second way is easier if you have a hard time reaching around to your back. With this method, you hold the bra upside down and inside out. Wrap the bra around you with the cups toward your back so you can fasten the hooks in front of you and then turn the bra around and finish putting it on. Now you can adjust the straps to make sure they are comfortable. If the bra feels too tight or loose around your back, simply adjust the hooks.

Breasts and Bras Dos and Don'ts

Whew! There is a lot of information to share at this puberty stop. If your brain feels a little swirly right now, don't worry. You can always come back and read this section again. For now, here is a short list of the most important things to remember about bras and breasts.

DO remember that your body is unique, and the timing of your breast development will be the right time for your body.

DON'T listen to anyone who tells you that they know more about your body than you.

DO find a bra that is comfortable and a good fit.

DON'T feel like you must wear a bra before you are ready.

DO measure, or get measured, so that you know exactly what size bra you should get.

DON'T try to figure it all out alone. It is more than okay to ask an adult.

DO ignore everything TV and movies tell you about having breasts; they are almost always wrong.

DON'T compare your breasts, or any other part of your body, with other girls'. You have different genes and your genes are great.

DO trust yourself and your body. You are practically an expert on it!

BELOW YOUR BELLY BUTTON

• •

Over the last few chapters we have stopped at several stations on the puberty track. From growth spurts to breast development, we have covered lots of ground. But there are still quite a few stops to go before we finish this ride. One of the changes that will be less noticeable—at least to the outside world—is the shift going on "down there" in your underwear. Here's what to expect.

THE HAIR DOWN THERE: PUBIC HAIR

We spent a little time talking about the hair that grows during puberty, including the hair on your arms, legs, and underarms. But one place you can expect to see more hair than you may be used to is on your genitals. The arrival of pubic hair often happens after breast development, but some girls (about 15 percent) may notice thin fine hair on their vulva and underarms before they have any signs of breasts.

Your body will decide which comes first. To best understand pubic hair, you should know the names of the parts "down there." Folks use all sorts of made-up names to talk about their private parts, which is okay, but it is equally important to know the official names. Here are some words and definitions that will make you an expert on the parts in your underpants.

VULVA: All the visible outside parts of your genital area

MONS PUBIS: The puffy mound of flesh just below your belly

LABIA: The inner and outer folds of skin on your vulva

LABIA MAJORA: The outer folds of skin on your vulva

LABIA MINORA: The inner folds of skin on your vulva

There are more parts to our genitals that we will discuss later. Now that you know the names of some of the most important areas, let's talk about pubic hair. In the beginning, your pubic hair may be very fine and thin, but as you go farther down the puberty line it will likely begin to grow thicker and darker. How much hair you get will probably be similar to the way your hair grows on other parts of your body, including your head, although most pubic hair will be thicker and coarser than the hair on your head. Pubic hair generally grows on the mons pubis and the outer labia first, and when it is fully formed will be the shape of an upside-down triangle.

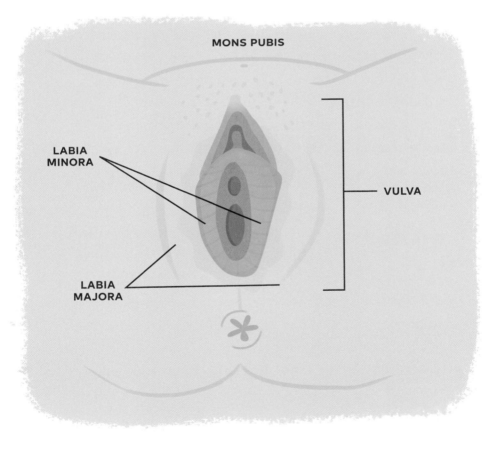

MONS PUBIS

LABIA MINORA

LABIA MAJORA

VULVA

Caring for Your Hair

Like other hair on your body, pubic hair should be taken care of. But don't worry, caring for the hair down there is easy. Earlier we discussed how bacteria and sweat can get trapped in our pubic and underarm hair and cause odor. The best way to keep odor and sweat under control in those areas is to shower daily, being mindful to dry off thoroughly and wear cotton underwear. Cotton is a material with tiny holes in the fabric that help keep you cool and dry. You should avoid using scented products on your vulva—the chemicals can cause irritation and sometimes infections. Bathing, drying yourself thoroughly, and wearing clean underwear will be the most important parts of caring for your pubic hair.

Swimsuits and Such

If you are worried about having your pubic hair peek out through your swimsuit, consider buying swimsuits that have swim short–styled bottoms. These bottoms come down the leg a bit farther and do a good job of covering pubic hair that may be growing down toward your thighs. For leotards, you can also use a small pair of fingernail scissors and clip the hair around the bikini line of your clothes. Some people use a shaving razor, but be sure to have an adult help you the first time you shave. You can get painful nicks, rashes, and razor bumps if you are not careful. There are some people who wax their pubic hairs, which involves using hot wax to rip the hairs out. Um . . . *ouch*! Remember, pubic hair is a natural part of puberty, and shaving or waxing it is not necessary at all. You can love your body and your body hair, too!

VAGINAL CHANGES

Pubic hair is not the only change that will happen to your genitals once puberty begins. Before we dive into these, let's finish our list of expert body words.

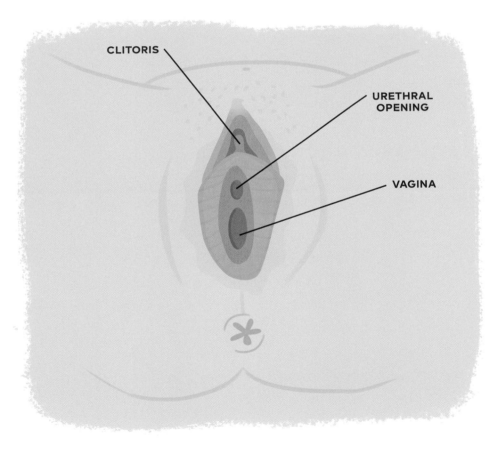

CLITORIS: The small, very sensitive bud of skin at the top of your labia

URETHRAL OPENING: The small hole below the clitoris where urine leaves the body

VAGINA: The canal and opening leading to your inside reproductive body parts. Discharge, menstrual fluid, and babies leave the body through this opening.

Knowing these words will help you understand the changes your body is going through during puberty.

Vaginal Discharge

About six months to a year before your first period you may discover white or yellowish stains in your underwear. What you are seeing is called vaginal discharge and is just another part of the puberty ride.

Vaginal discharge is a combination of mucus and fluid created by increased hormones in your body, and it is there to alert your body that soon you will begin your menstrual cycle. Want to know something really amazing? The vagina is a body part that cleanses itself. Cool, right?

Vaginal discharge is made of fluids produced by glands in the vagina that help rinse away unwanted bacteria. The thickness and color of vaginal discharge can change throughout the month depending on where you are in your menstrual cycle. Your discharge may be thin and clear, and other times it may be thicker and a little yellow in color. When discharge dries inside your underwear it may appear light brown. Having slight changes in your discharge is normal. Girls will continue to have discharge far into adulthood. Discharge usually lessens or stops when an older woman stops having a period (a stage called menopause).

Be a Discharge Detective

Vaginal discharge can tell you so much about what is happening inside your body at different points during the month. If you can identify when your discharge is regular, it will help you recognize when it may be irregular. Checking out your body is a great way to take care of your parts down there!

LIGHT YELLOW DISCHARGE: Seeing some yellow discharge when you wipe or on your underpants is normal, especially about a year or so before you get your first period. In fact, this type of discharge is a sign that your body is getting ready for your period.

WHITE, THICK DISCHARGE: This vaginal discharge is common at both the beginning and end of your period. If the discharge is clumpy, though—kind of like cottage cheese—you should talk to a trusted adult because it could be a sign of an infection.

CLEAR AND STRETCHY DISCHARGE: This is a sign that you're ovulating—releasing an egg.

CLEAR AND WATERY DISCHARGE: It's normal to see this type of discharge at any point during your cycle. You might even see a bit more of it when you're being more active, like when you're playing sports.

DARK YELLOW OR GREEN DISCHARGE: This color discharge could mean you have a vaginal infection, so be sure to ask an adult to take you to the doctor. But don't worry—most of these infections can be easily cleared up with some medicine.

BROWN DISCHARGE: This is usually a sign that the vagina is cleaning itself and getting rid of some old blood that might not have been cleaned out during your period.

Discharge often has a slight odor, which is natural. However, if your discharge is green or dark yellow, itchy, burns, or is painful in any way, you may have an infection. Because the vagina is a sensitive area of your body, it can be easy to get an infection—it doesn't mean you have done anything wrong. Using perfumed products, wearing damp swimsuits, or wearing tight clothing for too long can cause irritation or infections. Being aware of how your discharge looks normally will help you notice if something is off. If you notice any of the symptoms of a possible infection, you should talk to an adult or a doctor who can help you figure out the best way to treat the problem.

Some girls don't like the feeling of moisture between their legs or the occasional stains in their underwear caused by discharge. Using panty liners can be helpful. Panty liners are thin cotton strips that stick to the crotch of your underwear and help absorb moisture and keep your underwear stain-free (more on this in chapter 5). Remember, wearing clean cotton underwear and bathing each day is the best way to take fantastic care of your vulva, vagina, and all the other parts below.

YOUR PERIOD

. . . .

You have gone through lots of changes and growing to get to this point. So far, you know that during puberty your body will grow breasts that can one day produce milk and feed a baby. You have also learned how new hair will appear in places where you never had any before. You've even learned about discharge as a way the vagina cleanses itself as your body produces more hormones. These big changes have been preparing you to pull into perhaps the biggest station on this journey: The beginning of menstruation—also known as your period.

WHAT'S IT ALL ABOUT?

Menstruation is a sign from your body that it is growing, changing, and preparing itself to be able to become pregnant if you want to someday. Around the world, people have developed over 5,000 slang words for menstruation, including *period*, *Aunt Flow*, *crimson tide*, *lady days*, *that time of the month*, *Dot*, *red sea*, *monthly visitor*, *Mother Nature*, and *red moon*.

As you can tell, some are positive and some are funny, but many people simply describe it as getting your "period."

As mentioned earlier, in many cultures getting your period is a very special and important time in a girl's life. In others, it's just another interesting thing the body does. However you feel about your period is okay. What's most important is that you know what to expect and how to care for your body during your period.

GETTING READY

If puberty is going to be a beautiful train ride, one key to enjoying the journey is preparation. You've already taken one of the most important steps by reading this book to ensure you have accurate information—not just relying on someone at school who heard something from their sister who heard it from their aunt who heard it from the lady at the shoe store. Now it's time for more expert body words and definitions that describe your reproductive organs. Knowing these words will help you understand better the changes that are happening inside your body during this part of the journey.

UTERUS: A hollow, pear-shaped organ located in the lower abdomen; during pregnancy a fertilized egg will attach to the wall of the uterus and grow into a baby

OVARY: One of two sac-like organs where eggs are produced and stored in the body

OVA: The eggs stored in the ovaries

FALLOPIAN TUBE: Either of a pair of tubes along which eggs travel from the ovaries to the uterus

OVULATION: The release of an egg from the ovary for possible fertilization

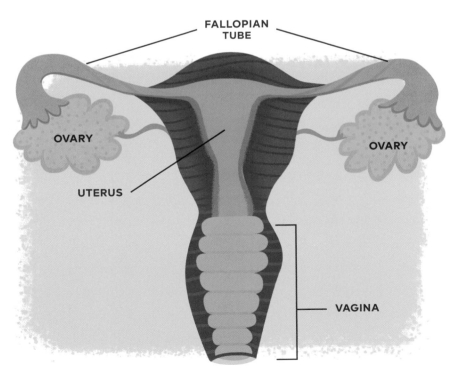

Estrogen and Your Ovaries

Since the beginning of puberty your body has been preparing itself for menstruation. It has been releasing a series of hormones necessary for keeping the puberty train running, and now, in order to be ready for menstruation, your body will need to release two powerful hormones: estrogen (which was mentioned earlier) and progesterone. The release of these hormones is how your body knows it's time to pull into menstruation station.

The Menstrual Cycle

Getting your period is the beginning of a process that takes about 28 days to complete and generally happens once a month. The period of time from the day you first see blood until you see blood again the next month is your menstrual cycle. While the average is 28 days, it is normal for you to take more or less time to go through this cycle. During the menstrual cycle, all your reproductive organs work together with the help of your hormones to prepare your body to make a baby someday. It takes a lot of work to grow a human, so your body basically prepares and practices every month, whether you ever have a baby or not.

Each month, your brain sends a message to your ovaries to start producing estrogen. Your ovaries, the two marble-size organs above your uterus, hold thousands of tiny ova (your eggs), and the production of estrogen is the signal that tells one ovary to release

Did you know all the eggs in your ovaries have existed there since you were born? They've been waiting their turn to one day be fertilized and become a baby or to get their special invitation to the period party!

one egg. The process of releasing an egg from the ovary is called ovulation.

Fallopian Tubes, the Uterus, and the Vagina

Once the egg leaves the ovary, it travels down one of the fallopian tubes on its way to the uterus. This is not a short journey. It can take three or more days for an egg to travel a little over an inch. If you were that tiny you would probably move very slowly, too! While the egg is on its road trip down the fallopian tube and you are going about your daily business of going to school, hanging out with friends, doing your chores, and finishing your homework, the hormone progesterone is helping your uterus (also known as your womb) grow a nutritious lining of blood, tissue, and protein just in case a fertilized egg appears. The uterus is where a fertilized egg would attach to the uterine lining, start absorbing the nutrients, and begin the process of growing into a baby. If the egg is not fertilized, your body sheds the egg and the uterine lining at the same time through your vagina. Once your uterus has squeezed out the lining during your period, your body begins making a new lining and the cycle starts all over again. That's pretty amazing!

How Long Is a Period and When Will I Get Mine?

When you start your period is another bit of secret information that only your body really knows. Girls often get their first period around two and a half years from the first sign of breast buds or about six months after they notice vaginal discharge. However, girls can start their period as young as 9 or as old as 16. Whenever you start is the perfect time for your body.

How long your period will last is also partly determined by your unique body. When you first start getting your period, it may be rather short, around three days or so, and the blood may be just a few pink, light red, or brownish spots in your underwear. Once your period becomes regular, it can be as short as two days or up to seven. It is also likely that your period will not come regularly in the beginning. Sometimes it can take up to six years for your period to become regular. This train is exciting, but can be a bit slow!

How Much Will I Bleed?

Girls can have light periods, heavy periods, or both. Even if a girl has a heavy period with what seems like lots of blood, most girls release only about two

"Denise already got her period. Geez, I'm gonna be 100 before I get mine!"

At this very moment, thousands of girls all over the world are having this conversation with themselves. Stomping around the house frustrated, thinking she is the last girl in her entire school to get her period. Here's what you need to know: Girls spend way too much time worrying about when they'll get their period or comparing the arrival with their friends'. Girls get their periods at different ages and times depending on what their genes, family history, and good old Mother Nature decides is best for them. For every girl, the period train will have its own schedule, and whenever it pulls into the station is just the right time!

tablespoons over the course of her period. You may have a little more or a little less. Some girls also get blood clots, which is thicker blood that sometimes comes out in chunks, kind of like jelly, which sounds a little gross, but all of it is normal.

Will Getting My Period Hurt?

Your period is the process of your uterus squeezing out its lining. That squeezing can feel like cramping below your belly button. Some girls may not feel much of anything when this happens, but for others it can be a bit uncomfortable. After all, your body doesn't use these muscles every day, just a few days a month, and sometimes those muscles get sore. It's like if you went on a long walk up a steep hill, your leg muscles might feel sore the next day. Many of the same things that would make your leg muscles feel better can help your uterine muscles feel better, too: a heating pad, a hot bath, and a little massage.

However, if you feel that you're in a lot of pain before or during your period (like it's hard to get out of bed or get through the school day), be sure to let a trusted adult know. This is something you might want to speak to a doctor about. After all, why should you suffer more than you need to?

My Period and PMS

Your body is so smart that it will often give you signals to let you know your period is on the way. These signs aren't the most fun, but they are your body telling you that it is gearing up for some hard and important work. A week or a few days before your period you may experience breast tenderness, feel a bit moody, feel heavier or bloated around your lower belly, and sometimes have cramps. These symptoms are called premenstrual syndrome (PMS).

Lots of girls experience these symptoms, and there are things you can do to reduce them. Eating right is a great way to help your body through PMS. It takes a lot of nutrients to make the uterine lining every month, so it's important to eat lots of healthy foods. Foods that contain calcium (yogurt, milk, and so on), iron (green leafy veggies and red meat), fiber (whole grains), and plenty of vitamins (fresh fruits and veggies) will help your body before, during, and after your period. Moving your body with light exercise and movement may also make PMS a little easier for you.

Does Period Blood Smell?

Period blood can have a mild odor, but no one can smell it through your clothes. No one will know you have your period unless you tell them. And as you learned earlier, washing daily and wearing clean underwear helps keep down smelly bacteria. This is true during your period as well. Changing your pad or tampon regularly (see page 79) can also help you feel fresh during your period.

Tracking Your Period

Another way to know when to expect your period is to track it. Your menstrual cycle begins on the first day of your period (the first day you see blood) in one month and runs to the first day of your period in the next month. The average cycle is 28 days, but it can be as long as 45 or as short as 21. On the first day of your period, draw a small heart on that day on your calendar. Draw a heart for each day of your period. After your

period is over, count the days until your next period begins. Begin counting from your first heart until your next period. That number of days is your cycle. Your cycle will take time to get regular, so the numbers may not be the same for a while. You can also use cool apps and websites to help you track your period so you know when it's coming. (See the links in the Resources on page 137.)

No matter when you get your first period, give yourself a high five when it arrives. Your body did some amazing work to get it here!

PERSONAL PERIOD CARE

Whew! That was a whole world of information. But we are not through. Now that you know what is happening in your body during your period, let's talk about care and hygiene during "that time of the month." Soon you will have all you need to know about pads, tampons, and more so that you can navigate menstruation with ease.

Pads, Tampons, and More

Companies make several products for period hygiene care, but the two most popular products are pads (also known as sanitary napkins) and tampons. Pads and tampons are both designed to absorb menstrual fluid.

A pad is a rectangular piece of material that sticks to your underwear and collects the blood as it leaves your body. Tampons are slender cylinders of cotton and other materials designed to absorb the blood while it is still inside your vagina. Some companies also make menstrual cups, which are small plastic or rubber cups that catch the blood inside your vagina. There are girls who prefer pads, others who prefer tampons, and still others who only use cups. There are even women and girls who use all three during their period. It will take time and practice to figure out which one is best for you.

How to Shop for Supplies

Most drugstores, grocery stores, and any place that sells body care products will have tampons and pads. Menstrual cups can be a little harder to find and a bit more expensive at first. You may need to go to a health food or natural products store to get them. Unlike pads and tampons that need to be replaced regularly, menstrual cups can last for years with good care.

Pads and tampons come in different sizes and absorbencies (how much fluid they can soak up) for heavy, regular, and light flows. Of course, companies also make all sorts of other styles, hoping that you will buy more.

How to Use Pads

Pads are made of cotton, plastic, and other materials that help soak up blood when you are having your period. There is sticky stuff on the backside that you press to the inside of your underwear to help the pad stay in place. Don't accidentally leave the sticky side facing up . . . *ouch!*

Once the pad is firmly in place you can pull up your underwear and get on with your day. You will need to change your pad a few times a day depending on how heavy your flow is. Pads are made in different sizes and with different absorbencies.

Below is a quick guide for what kind of pad you might need and how often you should change it.

DISCHARGE AND VERY LIGHT FLOW: Panty liners are good for these days. You should change your panty liner **about every 4 hours, or as needed**.

LIGHT TO MEDIUM FLOW: Regular or ultra-thin pads (the most commonly used pads) are good for these days. You should change your pad every **3 to 4 hours, or when you think it's necessary**.

HEAVY FLOW: Super, maxi, or overnight pads are best on days when your flow is heavy. Even if your flow is not heavy, using an overnight pad may help you feel more comfortable while you are sleeping. You should change your super or maxi pad about every **2 to 3 hours during the day, or as needed; overnight pads generally do not require changing before morning**.

Some pads have wings. These are small sticky tabs on the sides of the pad that wrap around your underwear. Wings keep your pad from slipping and help keep menstrual blood from leaking onto your underwear.

Getting Rid of Used Pads

Pads are disposable but cannot be flushed down the toilet. They can really clog up the plumbing! To properly dispose of your pad, roll it up with the sticky part on the outside. Once it is tightly rolled, wrap the pad in toilet paper and throw it in the trash. If you have a pet dog, be sure to put the used pad in a trashcan the dog cannot get into. Dogs seem to love used pads.

Some companies make washable and reusable pads. You can find websites where you can learn more about natural and reusable pads in the resource section at the back of the book.

How to Use Tampons

Many girls choose not to use tampons until they are older. Some girls don't feel ready or comfortable using something that goes inside their body when they first start their period. Whatever you choose is fine. You know what is best for your body.

A tampon is shaped like a cylinder and made of cotton and other materials that help it soak up the blood during your period before it leaves your body. It is connected to a long string that you use to pull the tampon out when it's time to change the tampon. Because a tampon catches the blood while it's still inside you, it is convenient for swimming or other activities for which a pad may be too bulky. You don't want to wear a pad in the pool because it absorbs water the same way it absorbs blood. That would be very uncomfortable!

Much like pads, tampons come in different absorbencies you can use depending on the heaviness of your flow.

SLENDER/SLIM/JUNIOR: These are good for very light flow. They are also a great choice to use for your first time because they are easier to insert.

REGULAR: These are for average flow and are the most commonly used.

SUPER: For heavy flow. You may need these occasionally, but they are not good to use in the beginning until you are used to inserting tampons.

SUPER PLUS/ULTRA: These are for very heavy days. Like super tampons, you'll want to use them only after you are used to inserting tampons.

You should always use the tampon with the lowest absorbency you need. Start with a slender or regular and then, as you get used to them, try the higher absorbencies if needed. You should change your tampon **roughly every 4 hours**. You may not have much blood on your tampon when you first start using them. That is okay. Change your tampon regularly anyway. It helps keep bacteria and odor away.

Some tampons have applicators to help you push them inside, while others have no applicator at all and you insert them using your fingers. Here's how to insert a tampon with an applicator.

How to insert a tampon with a built-in applicator:

1. First things first: Make sure you're doing this with clean hands. After washing and drying your hands, remove the tampon from the wrapper.

2. Most women prefer to stand when inserting the tampon. You can put one leg up on the toilet seat, or simply squat down a bit, while holding the tampon with your dominant hand (the one you write with).

TIP: If you are nervous, it may be difficult to insert the tampon because your muscles will be tight. Take a few deep breaths and try to relax before you begin.

3. Hold the spot in the middle of the tampon where the smaller, inner tube fits into the larger, outer tube (the applicator). Make sure the string is facing down (away from your body).

4. Place the tip of the outer tube into the vaginal opening. You can use your other hand to open your labia a bit to make it easier to insert the tampon.

5. Gently push the outer tube into the opening, guiding it toward your lower back. Stop when your fingers touch your body.

6. Once the outer tube is inside your vagina, use your index finger to push the inner tube through the outer tube.

7. Once the inner tube is all the way in, remove both tubes at the same time, place them in the used wrapper or roll them in toilet paper, and throw them away. (Don't flush them.) Make sure the string is hanging outside of your vaginal opening.

8. If you can feel the tampon inside you, or you are in any discomfort, then it wasn't inserted correctly. Remove the tampon by gently pulling on the string and start again.

9. Wash your hands again.

★ ★ TAMPON SAFETY ALERT ★ ★

While using tampons during your period is safe, it is important that you change your tampon regularly. You should never leave a tampon in your body for longer than eight hours or overnight. When a tampon is left inside the vagina too long it can increase your risk of developing toxic shock syndrome (TSS). TSS is a very rare bacterial infection that can make you very sick. If you experience dizziness, vomiting, diarrhea, a fever, or a rash that looks like sunburn, remove your tampon immediately, tell an adult, and see a doctor right away.

How to insert a non-applicator tampon:

1. Make sure you wash your hands thoroughly with soap and water. After drying your hands, unwrap the tampon.

2. Tug on the string to make sure the string is securely attached to the tampon.

3. Most women prefer to stand when inserting the tampon. You can put one leg up on the toilet seat, or simply squat down a bit, while holding the tampon with your dominant hand (the one you write with).

4. Make sure the string is visible and pointing away from your body.

5. With your other hand, open the labia and position the tampon in the vaginal opening.

6. Gently push the tampon into the opening, aiming for your lower back.

7. Once the tampon is inside your vagina, use your index finger to push the tampon in. Make sure that the string clearly hangs outside the opening to your vagina.

8. If you can feel the tampon inside you, or you are in any discomfort, then it wasn't inserted correctly. Remove the tampon by gently pulling on the string and start again.

9. Wash your hands again.

To remove your tampon, pull down on the string until the tampon is out. (It may be a little harder to pull out if there is not much blood on the tampon. Just keep pulling gently.) Even if there is only a little blood on your tampon, don't reuse it. Get a new one and start fresh. Most tampons are made to be flushable (though the applicators aren't), but you should always check the box to make sure. If you are unsure, wrap the used tampon in plenty of toilet paper and toss it in the trash.

Stains and Leaks and Keeping a Period Pack

Your period can be an unpredictable visitor, even if you're tracking it. Since you also cannot predict when your first period will arrive, it's a good idea to keep a small "period pack" with you. A period pack is a small pouch or purse filled with items you will need if you start your period unexpectedly. Carrying a period pack will help make sure that no matter when "Aunt Flow" arrives, you will be ready for company.

Here are some things you can keep in your period pack:

* Pads or tampons (a few of both)

* Small sandwich bags (to throw out used pads)

* Extra pair of "just in case" underwear

* A travel-size pack of flushable baby wipes (for messier moments)

Even the most prepared girl will sometimes have leaks during her period and get a bit of blood on her clothes. There is no need to panic. Periods are a regular part of having a body, and bloodstains are a totally normal (if annoying) part of having a period. If you get blood on your clothes at school, use a jacket or shirt (if you don't have one, ask to borrow a friend's) and wrap it around your waist so the long part covers your backside. Then ask a trusted adult or the school nurse to help you. The school nurse often has extra clothes for these exact situations. They really do happen to all of us!

To clean out bloodstains, use mild soap and cold water to scrub the stain until it lightens. Don't put the clothing in the dryer because it can cause the stain to "set." Ask your mom, sister, or another trusted adult to help you remove the stain.

THE MOON AND OTHER MYTHS

There are lots of myths about periods. Some of them are mysterious, and others are hilarious. Here are just a few:

BLOOD MOON

For a long time people believed that menstrual cycles followed the cycles of the moon. Maybe they believed this because the average menstrual cycle is 28 days and moon cycles are 29.5. However, studies show that the moon has no control over when your period starts or ends.

FRIEND OR FLOW

It has been said that if women spend lots of time together their periods will begin to arrive at the same time. While it might be fun to think your uterus can convince other uteruses to bleed when it says so, this is another myth. A recent study of thousands of women and girls who lived together found that they all continued to have their periods at different times.

SHARK TANK

True or False: If you go in the ocean during your period a shark may attack you because it can smell your blood.

Answer: False! It is totally safe to swim during your period. Sharks cannot smell you bleeding.

FEEDING AND FUELING YOUR BODY

· ·

You have been on a major voyage through the many changes your body will experience during puberty. This train ride has been filled with stunning views of your one-of-a-kind body. All along the way you have learned how to care for your body as it does the hard work of helping you grow. Do you remember the three biggest ways you can help your body feel good and stay strong as you are going through puberty? You guessed it: nutritious food, fun movement and exercise, and a good night's rest.

NUTRITION

Your body is on a once-in-a-lifetime journey of growing and changing. To make the ride on the puberty train a healthy one, you will need wholesome and nutritious food. Often when we hear the word *nutrition*, we think of being forced to eat the yuckiest foods. Luckily, nutrition doesn't mean suffering through endless meals with peas, or whatever you don't like. Eating nutritious food can mean enjoying delicious food as well. Good for you can taste good, too.

Getting the right nutrition can not only affect how you grow during puberty, it can also affect how early or late you start puberty. Not getting enough healthy food can keep your body from launching the necessary hormones to begin puberty. And eating too much unhealthy food can cause your body to begin puberty changes sooner than it is supposed to. Since getting nutritious food is such a big deal for growing bodies like yours, let's talk about how to fuel your body.

A Rainbow of Flavors

One easy way to make sure you're getting lots of the healthy food you need to help your body handle puberty like a champ is to eat a rainbow. Okay, just kidding—you are not going to eat an actual rainbow. That would be quite a feat!

Eating the rainbow actually means eating natural foods that make up the colors of the rainbow, which makes it easier to get the vitamins and minerals your body needs to develop through puberty. Here are the yummy colors you will want to see on your plate, and how they will help your body grow.

RED: apples, cherries, red cabbage, strawberries, tomatoes, watermelon.

Red foods can help you develop a sharp memory and healthy heart.

ORANGE/YELLOW: butternut squash, cantaloupes, carrots, mangos, oranges, pineapples, potatoes, sweet potatoes, yellow peppers.

Eating from the yellow part of the rainbow means getting the vitamins you need to have healthy eyes, heart, and immune system.

GREEN: asparagus, broccoli, Brussels sprouts, collards, cucumbers, green beans, green peppers, kale, peas, spinach.

Greens will help you have healthy teeth, strong bones, and sharp eyes.

PURPLE/BLUE: beets, blackberries, blueberries, dark beans, eggplant, figs.

Purple and blue foods will boost your memory and help your body stay strong as you age.

WHITE: ginger, mushrooms, onions.

White foods will help keep your heart pumping strong and healthy.

"But," you say, "what if I make a rainbow of orange cheddar potato chips, strawberry fruit snacks, and green apple gummy bears? Can that count as eating the rainbow?"

Well, friend, while those colors are found in the rainbow, you will probably get a bellyache and a trip to the dentist for cavities faster than you will get the nutrition you really need for your body. Nope, rainbow-colored junk food will not help the puberty train have a smooth ride. And foods that are high in sugar, fats, and salts can cause health problems as you get older.

This does not mean you can never eat chips, candy, or cake. They are fine in moderation, though they should never replace fruits, vegetables, and grains on the breakfast, lunch, or dinner table. Fresh natural food that is close to its original form is what will always be healthier for you. This means trying to avoid *processed foods*.

The best way to know if a food is processed is to look at its packaging. Foods that come in boxes and cans or contain powders, syrups, or other flavorings are usually processed. Processed foods often have had lots of sugar, salt, and fats added to them, while many of the nutrients have been stripped away. It is better to look for fresh food choices whenever you can. For example, a fresh peach is going to give you more nutrition than canned peaches in sugary syrup.

Your body will need a few other nutrients to keep it in tip-top shape. Foods with protein—like meat, fish, beans, and cheese—will help you develop healthy muscles. You will also need foods with iron in them for energy, zinc to help your body fight illness, and folates to help your body soak up needed minerals.

Be a healthy food helper! Ask the grown-up who does the grocery shopping if you can tag along and help them pick out delicious rainbow-colored fresh food. Tell them it will be good for your taste buds, as well as your rapidly growing body.

Start Your Day the Right Way

One of the best gifts you can give your brilliant body is breakfast. Eating breakfast each day is like saying, "Good morning, body! Glad to see you today!" Breakfast is perhaps the most important meal of the day. It gives your body the energy it needs to start running all those complicated functions that keep you alive. It also helps you not feel cranky and tired in the afternoon. Great breakfast ideas include oatmeal, fruit smoothies, eggs and toast, and bananas and peanut butter.

Allergies, Veggies Only, and Other Special Food Needs

People have different nutritional needs and their bodies react differently to food. Some people can't eat gluten (wheat products), and others have severe food allergies. Caring for our bodies sometimes means taking care of our special food needs. Food allergies—when foods cause a negative physical reaction in our bodies if we eat them (like itching, swelling, or other dangerous reactions)—are a common issue for many young people. In fact, up to three million people in the United States are allergic to some sort of food. Unfortunately, just because a food isn't good for your body doesn't mean it won't taste good. And this is where you can find yourself in trouble. Never eat foods you know you are allergic to, no matter how scrumptious they may look.

Hormone increases and stress during puberty can make allergies worse. So continue to eat healthy and be sure to stay away from foods that will trigger a reaction—your body will thank you!

Vegetarians are people who do not eat meat. People become vegetarian for many reasons, including religion and caring about animals. If you are a vegetarian or

★ ★ SPECIAL DIETS ★ ★ AND SPECIAL OCCASIONS

If you're going to a birthday party or a restaurant, let the adults in charge know about your special food needs in advance (whether you have allergies or are vegetarian). When you have special food needs, it can feel like you are left out of the fun, but that does not have to be the case. Learning what foods work best in your body is something to be proud of. It is a great way to care for yourself and to remind the world that there is more than one kind of body.

are considering becoming one, you'll need to figure out ways to get all the nutrition you need from other foods. You will need extra protein and vitamins (like B_{12}) that are mostly found in meat products. Talk with an adult and a doctor who can help make sure you are getting what your body needs to grow.

EXERCISE

One of the best ways to help your body is to move it! Exercise—getting up and moving around—is a wonderful way to support your ever-changing body.

Now that doesn't mean you need to do 300 jumping jacks and run 12 laps around the gym . . . unless you really like jumping jacks and running! But you should find ways to move your body that make you happy and sweaty. Do you love dancing? Ask your parent or a teacher to help you find a dance class. Or you can make up dance routines at home. Do you love sports?

Join your school's basketball, softball, or soccer team (or whatever sport you like). You could even get your friends in the neighborhood to play on weekends. There are endless possibilities for how to move your body. The important thing is that you get moving.

What Do I Get Out of Exercise?

Want to know how you build strong muscles and bones? Move them! Would you like to feel like you have lots of energy and focus and feel more relaxed and calm? Move your body! Exercise gives your body the energy and strength it needs to take this super journey through puberty.

How Much Do I Need to Move?

Most doctors suggest that you move at least one hour a day. If you are doing stuff you love to do, it will be easy to get to an hour. But remember, even a little exercise is better than none. If getting out and moving is hard because you haven't done it for a while, start small and work your way up. Try going for a walk with a friend for 20 minutes, or ask a neighbor if you can walk their dog. The more often you practice moving your body, the easier it is to do. If you have a disability that makes exercise difficult, try to think of exercises that work for your body and feel fun. Do them for as long as you can. Movement can look different for different bodies.

And for inspiration, here are 10 fun Move Your Body games to play at home!

1. **Headstands:** Strengthen your stomach muscles and get that blood to your brain by practicing a headstand.

2. **Jump rope:** Get your heartbeat going with this fun exercise. Go outside and get friends to join you.

3. **Wheelbarrow, crab, and bear-walk races:** You and your partner (you will need one) will build arm, leg, and stomach strength with these games.

4. **Animal races:** Bunny hop, frog leap, and quack around like a duck to see who can get the farthest.

5. **Obstacle course:** Create an obstacle course indoors with pillows, stuffed animals, and toys (just be sure to ask an adult before you start moving furniture). Or you can map a course outside with sidewalk chalk.

6. **Freeze dance:** Do your best moves and freeze when the music stops. Shake your tail feathers when the song comes back on.

7. **Bubble wrap attack:** Have a stomping good time jumping on the bubble wrap until all of the bubbles have popped.

8. **Clean-up race:** Grab a timer and set it for two minutes. See how fast you and a friend can clean up your room. Make it a race or just a fun helping game.

9. **Pillow fight:** Do it! It's awesome!

10. **Popcorn push-ups:** Put a small bowl of popcorn on the floor. Do a push-up near the bowl and stick out your tongue, trying to grab a bit of popcorn with each push-up you do.

Moving Your Body Safely

Our bodies are sturdy, but they are also delicate and need some care before we start moving them around. Warming up and cooling down are especially important if you play on a sports team or dance in a company; dancers and athletes may get injuries more often because of the stress both activities can put on muscles and bones.

It is important to warm your muscles up before you begin exercising. Warm-ups can include stretches, light walking, slow swimming, and any other easy movement that helps your muscles prepare for a workout.

You will also want to cool down after you exercise. Cool-downs help your body slowly return to a state of rest. Suddenly stopping during exercise can shock your muscles and cause soreness or more serious injuries. You will want to slow down your movement or return to stretching until you can feel your heartbeat slow down. Once your heart is beating more slowly and your breathing has slowed down, you can safely rest your body.

H2 Oh!

Guess what your body absolutely must have to live—water! Water is the most magical fluid in the world. Did you know that your body is made up of mostly water? So of course, your body is magic! Water is the best drink you can give your body, helping it continue to feel good and work properly.

Exactly how much water you should drink each day is up for some debate. But what we know for sure is that you should drink more water than any other drink. Sodas and juices often have tons of sugar and salt in them, which don't help your body work well when you drink too much of them. You should drink one to two glasses of water before you start exercising, a glass during your exercise, and at least one glass afterward.

If you wait to drink water until you are thirsty, your body is already low on the water it needs.

SLEEP

Whether you still love a bedtime story or you drift off to dreamland right when your head hits the pillow, one thing is for certain: Your body needs sleep and lots of it if you are going to stay healthy and happy during (and after) puberty. Your body is growing faster than at almost any other point in your life. New hormones are being made that will help your body begin all sorts of new functions, and these big changes take an enormous amount of energy. How do you make sure your body has what it needs to succeed at growing your great body? One very necessary way is by making sure you get enough sleep.

How Much Sleep Is Enough?

Girls between the ages of 8 and 11 years old should be getting between 9 and 11 hours of sleep per night. So to take good care of your body, you may need to miss the late shows on TV.

Why Do I Need So Much Sleep?

As your body prepares for puberty, you may notice yourself being sleepier than usual or having a harder time waking up in the morning. Needing more sleep is a normal part of puberty. Remember, your body is taking on some big new tasks like growth spurts (most bone growth happens while you sleep), producing hormones, and growing entire new body parts like breasts. That is a tremendous amount of work your body is doing, and it needs energy to do it.

If you don't get the sleep you need, it can affect your memory, ability to learn and understand, and mood. You simply don't want to be a cranky, exhausted, sleepy person for your spelling test. One of the best ways to make sure your brain and body are working in their best condition is to give them lots of good sleep.

Three Tips for Sound Sleep

Your days are probably pretty busy. You likely have
school, homework, activities, friends, family, and
chores. Whew! With so much going on, it can be hard
to wind down and turn off your brain so you can go to
sleep at the end of the day, even if you are tired. Here
are a few tips that will have you snoozing in no time:

1. **Have a Bedtime and Stick to It**
   Your body will be more ready to rest if it knows
   when to expect it. Having a specific time you go to
   bed each night will help make sure you're getting the
   hours of sleep you need.

2. **Stay Away from "Stay Awake" Foods and Drinks**

   Some foods and drinks have an ingredient that can increase your energy or make you feel jumpy and wide-awake. Eating or drinking them near bedtime will make it hard to fall asleep. Drinks like soda, coffee, and some teas, and foods like chocolate have an ingredient called caffeine that can make it difficult to fall asleep. You should limit how much caffeine you have each day and avoid it for at least five hours before bedtime.

3. **Lights Out**

   Our bodies are designed to wake up in the daylight and sleep at night. This is a pretty cool trick our bodies naturally do, and things like lamps, computers, and cell phone screens can easily confuse our bodies into thinking they should still be awake. Turning off the lights and the screens at least 30 minutes before bedtime is a great way to remind your body that it is time to rest and recharge.

What Won't Help

While nutrition, exercise, and sleep will help you keep the puberty train moving, there are three things that will leave you and your body stuck on the tracks—so just say no.

♥ YOU HAVE COMPANY! ♥

If you have trouble falling asleep at night, don't worry. You are not alone. From bad dreams to waking up throughout the night, scientists say between 10 and 33 percent of kids have issues sleeping.

Everyone has nightmares sometimes. They are not fun, but they can happen. Most nightmares are your brain processing something it is afraid of or worried about. If nightmares are keeping you from getting to sleep, mention them to an adult.

Try to avoid scary or violent television and games during the day because they can pop up in your dreams. Things like soothing music or nighttime stories with your parent can help you feel calmer at bedtime.

Some girls struggle with insomnia, which means difficulty falling or staying asleep. All sorts of situations can cause insomnia, such as worry or emotional stress (family or friend concerns), feeling sick or uncomfortable (if you have a sore throat, cough, or stuffy nose), or temperature (if your room is too hot or too cold). Most people get insomnia every once in a while. If you have insomnia that lasts more than a week or two, talk to an adult. A doctor can likely help you sort out what's in the way of you and catching the necessary ZZZs.

Smoking

Cigarettes were created to help companies earn tons of money from making you think smoking is cool. Companies get very rich convincing young people to start smoking early because they know cigarettes are addictive (once you start it is hard for your body to stop).

Here's what you need to remember: First, you are too smart to let some sneaky company take advantage of you for years. And second, just about everybody knows that cigarettes don't just make you cough and make your clothes and hair and breath smell gross—they can be deadly. Cigarettes cause cancer, lung disease, and all sorts of other life-threatening conditions. Don't let slimy companies cheat you out of your health or your money. Don't smoke!

Alcohol and Drugs

Billboards, commercials, and magazines are constantly talking about alcohol. TV shows and news programs are constantly talking about drugs. Why? For the same reason cigarette companies talk about cigarettes. Companies make lots of money when people buy and drink alcohol, and drug dealers make lots of money when people buy and use drugs.

Here's the deal: Drugs and alcohol are super dangerous for young people. Yes, they can be super dangerous for adults, too. But your body is changing and developing in serious ways during puberty. Alcohol and drugs can hurt that process and cause you problems all the way into adulthood. Both alcohol and drugs (including marijuana) can cause brain damage and hurt your kidneys, liver, and heart as they grow. Simply put, drugs and alcohol can cause you lots of harm.

Some kids try to make drinking, doing drugs, and smoking seem like the cool thing to do. Often kids do this because they don't feel good about themselves or because they are having problems in their life they don't know how to deal with. It's okay to find an adult you trust and talk about these feelings and issues. It's okay to ask for help. You don't have to go through any of the hard stuff alone. Growing up can feel overwhelming sometimes, but you have all the power and smarts inside you that you need to grow into a fantastic and brave young person—and you don't need drugs and alcohol to do it.

FEELINGS AND FRIENDS

· ·

You (and your body) have done some colossal
work to get you this far. Give yourself a fist bump!
You have learned a lot about your fascinating
and fantastic body. But bodies are not the only
things that change during puberty—you will also
experience emotional changes. Feelings, friends,
and ideas may also change during this time. Yes,
this is another puberty train station and everyone
with a body must stop here. Let's talk about what
to expect.

EMOTIONAL UPS AND DOWNS

While puberty is most definitely a train ride, on occasion it can feel more like a roller coaster with some high hills and steep drops along the way. Have you ever stormed off to your room because your mom said something you didn't like? Do you sometimes feel like your feelings are all over the place? A large part of what you're experiencing is the result of something we've talked about throughout this book. Any guesses? Go ahead, I bet you know. Yes! Good old hormones. Your body is producing new chemicals to help you grow ever so slowly into an adult. These hormones affect many of your body's functions, but they also affect your emotions.

Why Are My Feelings So Intense?

Humans feel things: Joy, sadness, anger, frustration, confusion, worry, wonder, excitement, fear, and a thousand other feelings we might not even have words for yet! Strong emotions are part of being human. As your body adjusts to the new hormones you are producing, you may notice that your feelings feel bigger than they have ever felt before. In some ways, they *are* bigger than they have ever been before. These feelings may make you more sensitive than usual. Some days you may feel like crying for no clear reason. At other moments you may feel super angry about something that used to just irritate you a little. All of this is normal and okay.

Of course, your changing feelings can be awkward and intense. It's possible you may also be experiencing new emotions like jealousy or even romantic feelings toward a friend or classmate. You may feel misunderstood or proud. You may have questions about yourself and the world that you never had before. The more experiences you have, the more feelings are possible.

No matter what feelings you may experience during this time, it is important to know that you are important and smart and capable. You are good enough, no matter what feelings show up. Always remember, feelings do not last forever. They change very quickly. Take a deep breath and stay on the train. It's just part of the ride.

How Can I Manage My Mood?

You may feel like your emotions are running the show and just dragging you along. But you don't have to hang on to the caboose on this train ride. There are things you can do to help manage your emotions during puberty. In fact, we already reviewed some of them in the last chapter.

Back to the Big Three

Eating healthy food will make your moods easier to handle. A sure way to feel cranky and frustrated is to let yourself get too hungry or to eat food that doesn't feel good inside your body. When you don't eat, your body gets slow and sluggish. As you lose energy your mood can also begin to go down. There is nothing worse than being hungry and angry at the same time—or what we call *hangry*. Don't be hangry. Eat three healthy meals and small healthy snacks throughout the day.

Exercise releases chemicals in your brain that make you feel good. Feeling frustrated? Take a walk around the block. Feeling sad? Try swimming some laps in your local pool or throw on some music and dance the happy back into your body.

And don't forget about sleep. Your mind and body need time to recharge. Sleep is like food for your brain. Your mind will get hangry if it doesn't get what it needs, which is 9 to 11 hours of sleep each night.

Meditation

Sitting quietly for a few minutes each day and letting your mind practice being quiet can also help your moods. This practice is called meditation, and it is a great tool for helping you cope when your emotions feel out of control. Meditation teaches you how to sit with your feelings until they leave. Feelings can be like houseguests who don't stay very long. They usually don't plan on moving in. (Check out YouTube for videos that help beginners learn about meditation.)

Talk or Write It Out

Having all these strong and new emotions can feel confusing. One way to lessen the confusion is to get the ideas out of your head. Talking about your feelings with a trusted adult who cares about you, believes in you, and wants the best for you is a wonderful way to move through tough emotions without feeling like you are alone. Find an adult who is a good listener and can talk to you about what you're feeling. They went through puberty too, and may have the right words to help you.

Another great way to let those feelings out is to write in a journal. Write down your fears, joys, and

successes. Write when someone makes you boiling hot with anger or when a friend hurts you. Write when your outfit is fabulous or when you think your classmates are judging you. Writing is an easy but effective way to let out your feelings in a safe place.

Maybe you can share your journal with someone you trust, or maybe it is just for you. Either way, writing can help you sort through the roller-coaster ride of feelings in a healthy way.

FRIENDSHIPS IN FLUX

Do you have a best friend? Perhaps you share secrets and hang out together. Maybe you have sleepovers and play games. You might talk to each other when things are hard and make each other laugh until you shoot milk out of your noses. You may even make each other angry and hurt each other's feelings—but you always say sorry and make up. It's possible you've even gone for days or weeks without speaking. Friendships are beautiful, but they are not perfect. Like anything you love, you must take care of your friendship if you want it to last.

Unfortunately, not all friendships last forever. There may be a few very special friends you keep forever, but most friendships shift and change as you shift and change. You may have a friend who has been your friend for years, but you may also have friends for a few weeks, a couple of months, or just the school year. As you get older and change, your friendships may change, too—and that's normal.

What Makes a Good Friend?

Whether you have the same friend for 20 years or just a short time, friends will be an important part of your life for the rest of your life. Humans need other humans, and that is part of the reason we make friends. We are wired to find people we like and spend time with them. Finding good friends matters, as does being a good friend.

Unfortunately, there are no written instructions on how to be a good friend, so we sort of stumble into the oops and ouches of these relationships. But we don't have to. Finding good friends doesn't have to be a mystery, but it does mean you have to be the kind of friend you would like to have. What makes a good friend? Here are 20 top qualities that make up a good friend:

A Good Friend . . .

1. doesn't want to hurt your feelings.

2. says sorry when they do hurt you.

3. wants to have you around.

4. enjoys helping you make more good friends.

5. encourages you.

6. treats you with kindness.

7. listens to you.

8. wants to help, even if they are not sure what to do or say in the moment.

9. admits when they are wrong.

10. likes it most when you're being your truest self.

11. doesn't gossip about you or others.

12. won't ask you to choose between them and other friends.

13. doesn't talk behind your back.

14. encourages you to do your best.

15. is honest.

16. stands up for you and their other friends.

17. tells you if something is dangerous or harmful.

18. laughs with you, not at you.

19. makes time for you.

20. tries to make you feel better when you're feeling down or worried.

Being a good friend is as important as finding good friends. Here's a bit of sad news: Sometimes you can do all of the things on this list and someone may still not want to be your friend. Let's say you have a BFF who has been your best friend since kindergarten, and now it's fifth grade and suddenly they don't want to be your best friend anymore. Ouch. Of course that might hurt your feelings, but it doesn't mean they are a bad person or that there is anything wrong with you. It just means you are both growing and changing. And as we change, who makes a good fit as a friend may begin to change, too. Getting older means discovering new interests and hobbies. We may find new things that are fun, but different from what our old friends like. This is simply one of the changes that sometimes comes with puberty.

How Do I Know If a Friendship Is Over?

Sometimes friends hang out less and less often. But not hanging out as often does not always mean you and your friend are not friends. It could mean they are very busy or something is happening in their home life. The best way to know what is going in a friendship is to ask.

♥ YOU HAVE COMPANY! ♥

One way to find new friends is to meet your friends' friends. And the best way to make that happen is to introduce your friends to one another—show them how it's done!

Introduce your school friend to a friend in the neighborhood, and perhaps she'll introduce you to her neighborhood friends, too. Invite friends from all different parts of your life—from school, the neighborhood, sports teams, after-school activities, and so on—to your birthday party and introduce them to one another. Say hello to your friends' friends when you're invited to their parties, and you may make a new friend that way!

Before you strike up the conversation, though, make sure you want to remain friends with them. It's okay if you don't; just keep spending time with other people and less time with your old pal. Once you know what you want, you can make time to have a talk.

Talking about feelings and friendships can feel uncomfortable at times, but one quality of a good friend is being honest. You can start the conversation by asking if things are going okay with them. Then share that you have noticed that you two don't hang out as much as you used to and you wanted to check in about it. Your friend may tell you they have been busy with schoolwork or their family. Or they may say they don't know why you haven't been hanging out together. Don't forget that friendships require effort from both people. If you want to stay friends but you are the only one trying, then it might not be a good relationship. No matter how it turns out, learning how to be a good communicator will help you well beyond puberty. Your communication skills may even save some friendships along the way.

Making New Friends

Humans need friends, which means that someone is probably looking for new friends at the exact time you are. The work is to find each other. This can be a bit hard if you are shy, but it's not impossible. School is a good place to make friends because there are lots of chances to reach out and introduce yourself. If your teacher asks you to work in pairs, ask a person you would like to get to know if they would be willing to be your partner. Ask to sit next to a new person during lunch or in the library. But school is not the only place to meet new people. You can find new friends at after-school activities, by hanging out with family members like cousins, and by getting to know your neighbors.

FAMILY AND OTHER SAFE SPACES

Every girl deserves a space where she can feel safe and cared for. In fact, every human deserves this. For lots of different reasons, that space can be difficult to find. But even when finding a safe space feels hard, there is one place where you can find it: Inside you. Yes, everything you need to go through puberty and grow into an amazing person is already inside you. That special sauce is called wisdom, and if you learn to listen closely it can guide you to the answers you need most. Listening to yourself will help you find wise people to answer your questions or give you support and encouragement when needed.

Here are some ways you can listen to that smart voice inside you and let it guide you to finding the resources and people you need to help you grow into an incredible young person.

FIND A FRIENDLY EAR

Throughout this book you have been told to find a trusted adult to talk to if you have questions or concerns. But you may be asking, "How will I know if someone is a trusted adult?" Good question! A trusted adult is, first of all, an adult. Lots of kids ask other kids questions about puberty and growing up. It is okay to talk to your friends about your feelings, as they may be having some of the same feelings. Just keep in mind that your friends are not the best people to ask about how your body and life will change during puberty. What do they know? They are on this brand-new journey just like you.

But a trusted adult already knows the answers because they have already taken the class. A trusted adult is someone who you know cares about you and wants you to be safe and healthy. You may not always like what the trusted adult tells you, but in your heart, you know they want what is best for you.

People who ask you to keep secrets from other adults are not trusted adults. People who do things that hurt you physically or emotionally are not trusted adults, and people who tease or say cruel things to you are not, either. For many girls, their trusted adult might be their mom or dad or an older sibling, but other girls may not have those people in their life. It is okay. Families, like bodies, can look different, and for some girls their trusted adult will be a teacher who really believes in them, a school nurse, or a doctor.

You can also have more than one trusted adult. You may want to talk about friendships at school with a teacher, but talk to the school nurse about your period. What is most important is that you know it's okay to have questions and that you can look around until you find the right person to answer them.

You might be saying, "But what if I feel nervous or embarrassed about asking a question?" Nervousness is completely okay, and it is very common. But it shouldn't prevent you from asking for help. You can use this book

as a way to get your questions answered. Just take it to your trusted adult and ask them to read the parts that you want to talk about. You can also start a question jar. Write down the question you have and put it in a jar. Ask your trusted adult to read the question from the jar, write the answer, and put the question and answer back into the jar. This is a good way to start conversations that you may feel nervous about.

Always remember that there is nothing about your body, puberty, or growing up that you should feel ashamed of. Your beautiful body is on a spectacular journey and every adult has had to take the journey, too. There are plenty of people to help you along the way.

ALWAYS GET CONSENT

Your body is yours and no one else's. That means you get to make decisions about your body, like who can touch it and who cannot. You don't have to hug or kiss people you do not want to. And people who want to touch you should always ask your permission first. It is okay to tell them they must ask for your permission— even family members. This is called *consent*. Consent means that we should always get permission before we do anything to anyone else's body. You can practice asking for consent by saying, *"Please ask my permission before you touch my body."* Practice saying the sentence in your mirror at home until you feel comfortable and strong. The more you practice getting and giving consent, the easier it will be to say this sentence to others when you need to. Of course, this works both ways, so you will also need to get consent before you touch anyone else's body.

STOP BODY TALK

Because your body is your very own, that also means no one has a right to talk about it in ways you do not like. In general, it is rude to talk about other people's bodies. If your mom, dad, aunt, sister, cousin, classmate, or even a stranger is talking about your body in a way that makes you uncomfortable, it is perfectly okay to ask them to stop. You can practice saying, *"It is rude to talk about people's bodies. Please stop."*

One place where this sentence can be very useful is at school. As your body develops during puberty, other girls (and sometimes boys) may make comments about these changes. Unfortunately, not everyone is taught to respect other people's bodies, which means you may have to teach them how. You can tell them you learned that commenting on other's bodies is not okay, and you want to share what you have learned with them. Just like that, you have become a body-positive ambassador! If someone continues talking about your body, even after you have asked them to stop, talk to a trusted adult who can help you figure out what to do next.

YOUR RIGHT TO PRIVACY

As you move into puberty, it's okay to ask for more privacy. Privacy may mean keeping a journal that no one else can read, closing your bedroom door sometimes, or asking to be left alone when you need some space. Privacy is helpful as you grow into a teenager, but you want to be sure that you don't shut out the people who care about you. If you need some

space because you are upset, be sure to talk about your feelings later. Communication is a part of becoming a powerful young person, and good communicators talk things out, even when it is tough.

PEER PRESSURE AND PUBERTY

One of the most incredible parts of puberty and growing up is learning who you are. Every day you are discovering what you love and what you think is ridiculous. Your taste in music, clothes, and friends may be totally different than it used to be. Every day you are becoming more magnificently you.

Becoming you can be confusing at times, too. It can feel like you don't really know who you are and what you like anymore because it is different from the past. During these times you may experience peer pressure, when your friends or classmates try to convince you to do things you may not want to do. Kids will say things like, "Come on, everybody's doing it," or "All the cool kids are doing it," or "If you really like me/if you're really my friend, you'll do it." "It" can be anything from going someplace you don't really want to go, to saying you have a crush on someone when you don't, to drinking, smoking, or doing drugs.

No one who really cares about you will ever pressure you to do something you don't want to do. Good friends and good people don't do that. Just like your body will grow at its own unique pace, so will your social interests. There is more than enough time to grow into the person you want to be, and there is no reason to move any faster than you are ready for. Staying true to yourself and being your very best self are what make you a strong, smart, powerful girl!

★ ★ STAYING SAFE ON ★ ★ SOCIAL MEDIA

What's gigantic and endless and never goes away? It's the Internet and whatever you post on it. Social media can be great. You can keep up with friends, see what your classmates are doing on the weekend, and post your favorite funny face pictures. But social media can also be dangerous if you don't use it responsibly. Those funny face pics you shared can be seen by anyone on the Internet anywhere in the world, and what you post on it stays forever.

Never post anything online that you would not want your parents, teachers, or other adults to see, because it is likely they will. And while you may use social media for fun, there are strangers on the Internet who are unsafe. Never post your location or any private information about yourself, and don't friend people you don't know in real life. If someone you met online gives you a weird feeling, trust that feeling and tell an adult immediately.

CONCLUSION

Congratulations! You rode the puberty train all the way to growing up station! You have learned so much about your body and all the changes you can expect over the next few years. I hope you feel smarter and more prepared to handle puberty. Most of all, I hope you have learned that you are already a phenomenal girl and puberty can't and won't change that. If anything, puberty can help you feel more confident and clear about what an awesome human being you are.

Don't worry about being like anyone else. Don't worry about being different. Difference is beautiful. Your growing up journey will be as unique and special as you are. It will have ups and downs. There will be days when you feel strong and capable, and there may be days when you feel overwhelmed and even a little scared. It's okay. We have all felt that way before. But you have everything you need, right inside you, to become an exceptional adult.

Be proud of yourself. Be proud of your growing body. You have taken a big step to learn so much important information about how it works and the changes to come. That is the sign of a bright and capable girl who is committed to taking good care of herself. You are well on your way to becoming the best version of yourself. Enjoy the ride!

GLOSSARY

Acne: when excess oil mixes with sweat and dirt, clogging the pores in your skin and becoming inflamed.

Areolae: the dark circles around your nipples.

Blackheads: when excess oil mixes with sweat and dirt, clogging the pores and turning a dark color. Blackheads are a form of acne.

Breast bud: the hard bump underneath your nipple.

Caffeine: an ingredient in certain foods and drinks that can make it hard for you to sleep.

Calcium: the mineral that gives your bones strength; without it you can develop serious bone diseases later in life.

Clitoris: small, very sensitive bud of skin at the top of your labia.

Consent: permission before we do anything to anyone else's body.

Dandruff: flakes of dead skin from your scalp.

Delayed puberty: when a girl starts puberty later than usual.

Dermatologist: skin doctor.

Discharge: combination of mucus and fluid created by increased hormones in your body.

Estrogen: a hormone that is in charge of menstruation, as well as other body functions.

Fallopian tubes: the pair of tubes along which eggs travel from the ovaries to the uterus.

Genitals: your private area.

Growing pains: common aches and pains in your muscles, legs, and thighs that come and go as you experience a growth spurt.

Growth spurt: a time of rapid growth when your arms, legs, feet, and hands all get bigger.

Hormones: chemicals in your body that are important for the changes experienced during puberty.

Insomnia: difficulty falling or staying asleep.

Labia: inner and outer folds of skin on your vulva.

Meditation: the practice of sitting quietly for a few minutes each day and letting your mind practice being quiet.

Menopause: when an older woman stops menstruation.

Menstruation: part of a 28-day cycle in which blood and the lining of the uterus is shed and released from your vagina.

Myopia: nearsightedness.

Nipples: the buttons of skin on top of your aerolae.

Ova: the eggs stored in the ovaries.

Ovary: one of two sac-like organs where eggs are produced and stored in the body. The ovaries produce hormones that signal that it's time for all the other changes to start.

Ovulation: when your body releases an egg before your period.

Peer pressure: when your friends or classmates try to convince you to do what you really don't want to do.

Precocious puberty: when a girl starts puberty before her body is ready for it.

Premenstrual syndrome (PMS): symptoms a girl may experience a week or a few days before her period, including tenderness, moodiness, heaviness or bloating around the lower belly, and cramping.

Puberty: the age at or time during which the body matures and becomes capable of reproducing.

Pubic mound (mons pubis): the puffy mound of flesh just below your belly.

Scoliosis: a curve in the spine.

Urethral opening/Urethra: the small hole below the clitoris where urine leaves the body.

Uterus: the hollow, pear-shaped organ located in the lower abdomen.

Vagina: the canal and opening leading to your inside reproductive body parts.

Vulva: all the visible outside parts of your genital area.

RESOURCES

Puberty is a process and this book is just the beginning. In addition to all the information in this book, the following are resources that can help you on your puberty journey.

Introduction

Print Books

Wong, Wallace. *When Kathy is Keith*. Xlibris, 2011.

Herthel, Jessica. *I Am Jazz*. Dial Books, 2014.

Online Resources

Amaze:
https://amaze.org/?topic=gender-identity
Amaze.org shares resources on gender identity and questions.

Trans Youth Equality:
www.transyouthequality.org
Trans Youth Equality shares resources and support for transgender and gender questioning youth.

Chapter 1

Print Books

Dunham, Kelli. *The Girl's Body Book: Fourth Edition.*
Kennebunkport, Maine: Applesauce Press, 2017.

Online Resources

BodyPositive:
http://www.bodypositive.com/childwt.htm
BodyPositive looks at ways we can feel good in the
bodies we have.

Center for Young Women's Health:
https://youngwomenshealth.org
The Center for Young Women's Health (CYWH) is a
partnership between the Division of Adolescent/Young
Adult Medicine and the Division of Gynecology at Boston
Children's Hospital. The Center is an educational entity
that is committed to providing teen girls and young women
with carefully researched health information, educational
programs, and conferences.

Girls' Health:
https://www.girlshealth.gov/
Girlshealth.gov offers information on health and well-being.
The site covers hundreds of topics, from getting your period
to stopping bullies, and from exercise to safety.

Chapter 2

Print Books

Beaumont, Mary R. *The Hair Book: Care & Keeping Advice for Girls.* Middleton, WI: American Girl Publishing, Inc., 2016.

Taylor, Julia V. and Melissa A. Wardy. *The Body Image Workbook for Teens: Activities to Help Girls Develop a Healthy Body Image in an Image-Obsessed World.* Oakland, CA: Instant Help, 2014.

Zelinger, Laurie and Jennifer Kalis. *A Smart Girl's Guide to Liking Herself, Even on the Bad Days.* Middleton, WI: American Girl Publishing, Inc., 2012.

Online Resources

Association for Size Diversity and Health:
https://www.sizediversityandhealth.org
ASDAH is a nonprofit organization committed to the practice of the Health At Every Size Principles. ASDAH envisions a world that celebrates bodies of all shapes and sizes, in which body weight is no longer a source of discrimination and where oppressed communities have equal access to the resources and practices that support health and well-being.

Shawntas Way YouTube Channel:
https://www.youtube.com/channel/UCvM7efGeikAsDnsBr3MmL5g
"How I Grew My Long Natural Hair"
"How to Moisturize and Twist Out Little Girls' Natural Hair"
"7-Year-Old Styles Her Own Hair"

Supa Natural YouTube Channel:

https://www.youtube.com/channel/UCvmHAtsWzrtHAaCQF8AoDHQ

"Tips and Tricks: Box Braid like a Professional"

"Triangle Part Braids"

"Quick Easy Hairstyle for 4c Hair Girls"

Chapter 3

Print Books

Jukes, Mavis. *Growing Up: It's a Girl Thing: Straight Talk about First Bras, First Periods, and Your Changing Body.* New York: Alfred A. Knopf, 1998.

Chapter 4

Print Books

Lavender, Missy, Jenifer Donatelli Ihm, and Jan Dolby. *Below Your Belt: How to Be Queen of Your Pelvic Region.* Chicago, IL: Women's Health Foundation, 2015.

Metten, Shelley. *I'm a Girl: My Changing Body.* Anatomy for Kids, LLC, 2013.

Chapter 5

Print Books

Gravelle, Karen. *The Period Book: A Girl's Guide to Growing Up.* New York: Bloomsbury USA Childrens, 2017.

Online Resources

Always Period Calendar

https://always.com/en-us/period-calculator

The Always period-tracking tool helps map out your cycle
for months.

MagicGirl

https://magicgirl.me

MagicGirl is the first period-tracker app for teens
and tweens.

Natural and Reusable Pads

New Moon Pads: https://www.newmoonpads.com

Homestead Emporium: http://homesteademporium.com

LunaPads: https://lunapads.com

Party In My Pants: https://partypantspads.com

There are many places that offer and sell reusable pads.
Do your own research about what is going to work best for
you. This is meant to be a starting place—but all bodies are
different and you'll have to discover the pads that work best
for you and your body!

Chapter 6

Print Books

Maring, Therese K. and Brenna Hansen. *A Smart Girl's Guide:
Sports & Fitness: How to Use Your Body and Mind to Play and
Feel Your Best.* Middleton, WI: American Girl, 2018.

Online Resources

Girls on the Run

https://www.girlsontherun.org

Girls on the Run is a nonprofit organization dedicated to creating a world where every girl knows and activates her limitless potential and is free to boldly pursue her dreams. Running is used to inspire and motivate girls, encourage lifelong health and fitness, and build confidence through accomplishment.

Chapter 7

Print Books

Flynn, Lisa. *Yoga for Children*. Avon, MA: Adams Media, 2013.

Grossman, Laurie. *Master of Mindfulness: How to Be Your Own Superhero in Times of Stress*. Oakland, CA: New Harbinger Publications, Inc., 2016.

Madison, Lynda and Masse Josee. *The Feelings Book: The Care and Keeping of Your Emotions*. Middleton, WI: American Girl, 2013.

Snel, Eline. *Sitting Still Like a Frog: Mindfulness Exercises for Kids*. Boston, MA: Shambhala Publications, Inc., 2013.

Online Resources

KidsHealth

http://kidshealth.org/en/kids/feeling

Confused, sad, mad, glad? Check out this KidsHealth section to learn about these emotions and many more—and how to deal with them.

Mindfulness

There are many great resources for meditation and mindfulness. Here are a few YouTube videos to get you started.

Fablefy Living Mindfully—Body Scan Meditation for Teens and Adults/Mindfulness For Children
https://www.youtube.com/watch?v=X462QPGZQt4

Fablefy Living Mindfully—3-Minute Body Scan Meditation
https://www.youtube.com/watch?v=ihwcw_ofuME

Meditation Channel—Breath Meditation for Kids
https://www.youtube.com/watch?v=CvF9AEe-ozc

GoZenOnline—Mindful Minute: Quick Mindfulness Meditation Exercise
https://www.youtube.com/watch?v=ZMEOJKiweL4

GoZenOnline—Body Scan Meditation
https://www.youtube.com/watch?v=aIC-lo441v4

Chapter 8

Online Resources

Blue Seat Studios YouTube Channel
Consent for Kids
https://www.youtube.com/watch?v=h3nhM9UlJjc

REFERENCES

Chapter 1

"All About Puberty." *KidsHealth*. Nemours Foundation. Last updated October 2015. http://kidshealth.org/en/kids/puberty.html.

Cooke, Kaz. *Girl Stuff 8-12*. Penguin eBooks, 2016.

Shroff, Amita. "Girls and Puberty." *WebMD*. WebMD, LLC. March 20, 2016. https://teens.webmd.com/girls/facts-about-puberty-girls#2.

"What to expect when your breasts bud." *Girlology & Guyology*. www.girlology.com/what-expect-when-your-breasts-bud. Accessed 24 Jan. 2018.

"World Demographics Profile 2018." *Index Mundi*, January 20, 2018. www.indexmundi.com/world/demographics_profile.html.

"World Population Prospects 2017." United Nations.
https://esa.un.org/unpd/wpp. Accessed 24 Jan. 2018.

Chapter 2

"5 Signs You May Need Braces." 1st Family Dental.
https://blog.1stfamilydental.com/5-signs-may-need-braces
Accessed 24 Jan. 2018.

"A Puberty Timeline for Girls." *Girlology & Guyology.*
https://www.girlology.com/puberty-timeline-girls.
Accessed 24 Jan. 2018.

"Average Human Grows 590 Miles of Hair and Eats 35 Tons of
Food . . . AMAZING Human Stats." *Daily Express.* October 17,
2013. www.express.co.uk/news/weird/437344/Average
-human-grows-590-miles-of-hair-and-eats-35-tons-of-food
-AMAZING-human-stats.

Burhenne, Mark. "What Is Plaque and Why Is It Harmful?"
Ask the Dentist. https://askthedentist.com/what-is-plaque.
Accessed 24 Jan. 2018.

"Calcium." *Center for Young Women's Health.* Last updated
January 5, 2017. https://youngwomenshealth.org/2013
/10/17/calcium.

Dahl, Andrew A. "Eye Diseases and Conditions." *MedicineNet.
com.* September 17, 2009. https://www.medicinenet.com
/image-collection/nearsightedness_picture/picture.htm.

Eddis, Yolanda. "Oral Health in Children as They Become Teenagers." *Colgate*. Colgate-Palmolive Company. www.colgate.com/en-us/oral-health/life-stages/teen -oral-care/oral-health-in-children-as-they-become -teenagers-0913. Accessed 24 Jan. 2018.

"Genetics Home Reference." *U.S. National Library of Medicine*. January 23, 2018. https://ghr.nlm.nih.gov/primer /basics/gene.

Grayson, Charlotte E. "Myopia." *MedicineNet.com*. WebMD Medical Reference. https://www.medicinenet.com/myopia /article.htm. Accessed 24 Jan. 2018.

"Growing Pains." *Women's and Children's Health Network*. Government of South Australia. July 13, 2017. http://www.cyh.com/HealthTopics/HealthTopicDetails .aspx?p=114&np=304&id=1520.

Hirsch, Larissa. "The Basics of Braces." *KidsHealth*. Nemours Foundation. March 2016. http://kidshealth.org/en/parents /braces.html.

"How Much Sun Is Enough?" *SunSmart*. Cancer Council Victoria. www.sunsmart.com.au/uv-sun-protection /how-much-sun-is-enough. Accessed 24 Jan. 2018.

Konie, Robin. "Your Body Needs Fat. Learn Why." *Thank Your Body*. www.thankyourbody.com/why-your-body-needs-fat/. Accessed 24 Jan. 2018.

Lamb, Philina. "Checkup on Health." *UC Davis Health*. www.ucdmc.ucdavis.edu/welcome/features/20090909 _teen_acne. Accessed 24 Jan. 2018.

Matz, Judith. "9 Common Mistakes Parents Make About Their Kids' Weight." *The Body Is Not an Apology.* November 11, 2017. https://thebodyisnotanapology.com/magazine/9-common -mistakes-parents-make-about-their-kids-weight.

"Nail Care: Grooming, Manicures & Problems." *Sutter Health.* Palo Alto Medical Foundation. www.pamf.org/teen/health /skin/nails.html. Accessed 24 Jan. 2018.

Page, Max. "Bearded Woman Beats the Bullies, Says Facial Hair Makes Her Feel 'Beautiful'." *Popdust.* February 19, 2014. www.popdust.com/bearded-woman-beats-the-bullies-says -facial-hair-makes-her-feel-beauti-1889836686.html.

"Puberty: Adolescent Female." *Stanford Children's Health.* www.stanfordchildrens.org/en/topic/default?id=puberty -adolescent-female-90-P01635. Accessed 24 Jan. 2018.

"Tips for Taking Care of Your Skin." *KidsHealth.* Nemours Foundation. http://kidshealth.org/en/teens/skin-tips.html. Accessed 24 Jan. 2018.

Quinn, Jessie. "Teens and Skin Care: How Puberty Can Affect Your Skin." *Skincare.* L'Oreal USA. June 24, 2016. www.skincare.com/article/teens-skin-care-how-puberty -can-affect-your-skin.

Shroff, Amita. "Girls and Puberty." *WebMD.* WebMD, LLC. March 20, 2016. https://teens.webmd.com/girls/facts-about -puberty-girls#1. Accessed 24 Jan. 2018.

Stoppler, Melissa C. "Puberty." *MedicineNet.com.* MedicineNet. August 1, 2016. www.medicinenet.com/puberty /article.htm.

"Sweating and Body Odour." *Women's and Children's Health Network*. December 12, 2016. www.cyh.com/HealthTopics /HealthTopicDetailsKids.aspx?p=335&np=289&id=3049.

"What Is Scoliosis?" *KidsHealth*. Nemours Foundation. http://kidshealth.org/en/teens/scoliosis.html. Accessed 24 Jan. 2018.

Chapter 3

"What to expect when your breasts bud." *Girlology & Guyology*. www.girlology.com/what-expect-when-your -breasts-bud. Accessed 24 Jan. 2018.

Chapter 4

Fsuyker [Mirella Di Persio]. "First Vaginal Discharge: What Teens Should Know." *The Healthy Vagina*. Multi-Gyn. January 9, 2014. www.healthyvagina.com/?p=758.

"What's Vaginal Discharge?" *KidsHealth*. Nemours Foundation. Last updated January 2015. http://kidshealth .org/en/kids/discharge.html.

Chapter 5

"All About Menstruation." *TeensHealth*. Nemours Foundation. http://kidshealth.org/en/teens/menstruation.html#. Accessed 24 Jan. 2018.

"Liner FAQs." *U by Kotex.* Kimberly-Clark Worldwide, Inc., www.ubykotex.com.au/femcare-products/liners/faqs. Accessed 24 Jan. 2018.

Lunapads. Lunapads.com. 2018. https://lunapads.com. Accessed 24 Jan. 2018.

MacMillen, Hayley. "Does the Moon Affect Your Period?" *Refinery29.* June 20, 2016. http://www.refinery29.com /2014/07/71005/full-moon#slide-5.

"Medical Definition of Uterus." *MedicineNet.com.* MedicineNet. May 13, 2016. www.medicinenet.com/script /main/art.asp?articlekey=5918.

"Pads and Tampons." *KidsHealth.* Nemours Foundation. Last updated January 2014. http://kidshealth.org/en/kids /pads-tampons.html.

Sargis, Robert M. "An Overview of the Ovaries." *EndocrineWeb.* Vertical Health, April 8, 2015. https://www .endocrineweb.com/endocrinology/overview-ovaries.

"Using Your First Tampon." Center for Young Women's Health, Boston Children's Hospital. July 25, 2016. https://youngwomenshealth.org/2012/09/27/tampons.

"When to Talk to Your Daughter Regarding First Period." *Sofy.* Unicharm Corporation. https://in.sofyclub.com/en/advice /forparents/05.html. Accessed 24 Jan. 2018.

Winters, Leigha. "Tampons." *Sutter Health*. Palo Alto Medical Foundation. Last reviewed October 2013. www.pamf.org/teen/health/femalehealth/periods /tampons.html.

"Your First Period (Especially for Teens)." *Frequently Asked Questions Especially for Teens*. American College of Obstetricians and Gynecologists, May 2015. www.acog .org/Patients/FAQs/Your-First-Period-Especially-for -Teens#menstrual.

Chapter 6

Adams, Lawrence. "Does Nutrition Affect Puberty." *Livestrong.com*. Leaf Group Ltd. June 13, 2017. www.livestrong.com/article/540730-does-nutrition -affect-puberty.

Bordessa, Kris. "18 Get-Off-the-Couch Games." *Parenting. com*. Meredith Corporation. http://www.parenting.com /gallery/18-fun-active-indoor-activities?page=9. Accessed 27 Jan. 2018.

Brittney, Lynn. "Teenager's Problems with Allergies." SafeKids. May 13, 2012. www.safekids.co.uk /teenagersallergyproblems.html.

Carter, Kevin A., Nathanael E. Hathaway, and Christine F. Lettieri. "Common Sleep Disorders in Children. *American Family Physician 89*, no. 5 (2014): 368-77. https://www.aafp .org/afp/2014/0301/p368.pdf. Accessed 27 Jan. 2018.

DeCesare, Leah. "6 Sleep Tips for Tweens and Teens." Mother's Circle, LLC. http://motherscircle.net/6-sleep-tips -for-tweens-and-teens. Accessed 27 Jan. 2018.

"Common Sleep Problems." *KidsHealth*. Nemours Foundation. Last reviewed August 2014. http://kidshealth.org/en /teens/sleep.html.

"Exercise Safely." *Women's and Children's Health Network*. Government of South Australia. October 23, 2017. www.cyh.com/HealthTopics/HealthTopicDetailsKids .aspx?p=335&np=285&id=1455.

Fader, Anna. "25 Exercise Games and Indoor Activities to Get Kids Moving." Mommy Poppins. February 17, 2016. https://mommypoppins.com/newyorkcitykids/25-exercise -games-indoor-activities-for-kids.

Friedlander, Whitney. "Nutrition for Kids During Puberty." *Mom.me*. Whalerock Digital Media LLC. December 6, 2012. https://mom.me/lifestyle/4907-nutrition-kids-during -puberty.

Henderson, Laura W. "Food and Vitamins for Puberty." *Livestrong.com*. Leaf Group Ltd. October 3, 2017. https://www.livestrong.com/article/112085-physical -development-adolescence.

Holecko, Catherine. "Fitness During Puberty." *Verywell.com*. Very Well Family. Last updated December 21, 2017. www.verywell.com/fitness-during-puberty-1257328.

Stang, Jamie, and Mary Story. *Guidelines for Adolescent Nutrition Services.* Center for Leadership, Education and Training in Maternal and Child Nutrition, Division of Epidemiology and Community Health, School of Public Health. University of Minnesota, 2005.

"Tween Sleep Facts." *Family Education.* Sandbox Networks, Inc. https://www.familyeducation.com/life/preteen -tween-sleep/tween-sleep-facts. Accessed 27 Jan. 2018.

Chapter 7

"Tips for Managing Your Emotions." *Lil-Lets Teens.* Lil-Lets UK Limited. http://www.becomingateen.co.uk/advice-blog /articles/managing-your-emotions. Accessed 27 Jan. 2018.

INDEX

ACKNOWLEDGMENTS

Reliving the raucous road of puberty through this book was quite the journey. I pray the work makes it possible for at least one girl to grow up without a body-shame origin story. This journey could not have been possible without the kindness of my new community in Aotearoa, New Zealand. Thank you to Alina and Mandy, Rod and Lyn, Matthew and Brian, and Anna for housing me in quiet beautiful spaces that gave me the room to complete this work while in New Zealand. Thank you to Kiterangi Cameron for cheerleading me along and for teaching me the Te Reo Maori word for book, *pukapuka*. I am beyond grateful for my family and friends who helped me feel a little less alone through the wizardry of technology via video chats and Marco Polo. Finally, thanks to the millions of girls who wake up every day and practice loving themselves in a world that does not always make it easy. I love you radically!

ABOUT THE AUTHOR

SONYA RENEE TAYLOR is the Founder and Radical
Executive Officer of TheBodyIsNotAnApology.com,
a digital media and education company committed
to radical self-love and body empowerment as
the foundational tool for social justice and global
transformation. Sonya is also an international
award-winning peformance poet, activist, speaker,
and transformational leader whose work continues
to have global reach. She has appeared across the
United States, New Zealand, Australia, England,
Scotland, Sweden, Germany, Brazil, Canada, and the
Netherlands. Sonya and her work have been seen,
heard, and read on HBO, BET, MTV, TV One, NPR,
PBS, CNN, Oxygen Network, *New York Times*, *New
York* magazine, MSNBC.com, Today.com, Huffington
Post, *Vogue Australia*, Shape.com, *Ms.* Magazine,

and many more. She currently resides in California and New Zealand, where she is an inaugural fellow in the Edmund Hillary Fellowship for global impact change-makers. You can learn more about her radical self-love work at SonyaReneeTaylor.com and TheBodyIsNotAnApology.com.

CELEBRATE YOUR
FEELINGS

CELEBRATE YOUR
FEELINGS

THE POSITIVE MINDSET
PUBERTY BOOK FOR GIRLS

BY LAUREN RIVERS, MS

Illustrated by CAIT BRENNAN

ROCKRIDGE
PRESS

Interior and Cover Designer: Tricia Jang
Art Producer: Hannah Dickerson
Editor: Eun H. Jeong
Production Editor: Emily Sheehan
Illustrations © Cait Brennan
Decorative patterns courtesy of Shutterstock
Author photo courtesy of Clark Douglas

ISBN: Print 978-1-64739-289-5 | eBook 978-1-64739-290-1

R0

TO MY MOM,
who, due to her unconditional
support, constant listening ear, and
kind spirit, has taught me more about
what it takes to be a counselor than
any course or textbook.

TO MYRA,
for loving us as your own.

AND TO ANY GIRL
wondering whether things gets better—
they most certainly do.

CONTENTS

Dear Reader,

You may not realize it, but every day you are changing and growing. When you were younger, you might have felt scared when someone yelled, but maybe now you feel angry. Or maybe you once loved to sing in front of people, but now you feel shy or want to run and hide from attention. These new feelings can leave you confused or with a lot of questions. I remember being VERY confused!

When I was your age, I experienced all kinds of emotions. Sometimes it felt like a roller coaster as my feelings soared from sad to joyful to angry— sometimes all in a single day. (Can you relate to this?) During puberty, I got a lot of advice from parents and teachers on how my body was changing, but nobody talked to me about all the changes I was experiencing inside of me. I wasn't sure if what I was going through was normal. I was nervous, but also curious.

My curiosity continued to grow, and I decided to study clinical mental health counseling at Johns Hopkins University and to work in elementary schools, offices, and hospitals in Baltimore, Maryland, and Northern Virginia. And now my job is to help adolescents like you navigate through these social and emotional changes. I love my job, and I've met some amazing young girls. As I help them, I learn so much from them, too. It's been a lot of fun. Now, I'm excited to take all that I've learned and put it in the book you're holding!

This book will help you feel excited for these amazing changes and will teach you super-helpful skills to manage your emotions, relationships, thoughts, and moods. By the end of this book, I believe you will know yourself and appreciate yourself better. You'll also have what it takes to connect with others as a strong, smart, and confident person.

I look forward to joining you on this new adventure!

Yours truly,
Lauren Rivers

MY CHANGING EMOTIONS

You are unique. You are special. You are awesome. Uncertainty about your feelings might keep you from seeing that, and that's normal! The more you understand your feelings and emotions, the less confused you will feel as you grow and change. You may not realize it, but you already have everything you need inside you to handle these changes. But certain tools and tricks can make it much easier— and that's where this book comes in.

Have you ever burst into tears or stomped your feet when someone made you angry? Did you ever feel like you were about to cry in class and tried your hardest to stop yourself? Your feelings might be different from those of a family member, best friend, or favorite teacher. That's okay! There's no limit to how many emotions you can feel, and there's no right or wrong way to have them, either. Have you ever wondered why you cover your eyes or jump during the scary part of a movie? Well, your feelings affect how your body reacts! Pretty neat stuff, huh? But our feelings don't just affect our body—they also impact the way we see ourselves, treat our friends, and experience the world around us.

WHAT AM I FEELING?

Think of yourself as the captain of your emotions, on a boat in a big, beautiful sea of growth and change. Your feelings are a lot like waves. Sometimes feelings can be huge, choppy, scary waves. Sometimes you're happy because the waves are small and smooth—of course, this is when it's easier to navigate the boat.

Emotions and feelings are words that help describe how we feel on the inside. We have emotions and feelings all day long. Some emotions are nice and can make us feel warm and fuzzy, like excitement. Others, like anger, are tougher, and we may try to ignore them. Emotions are our response, or our reaction, to things that happen to us. Our emotions create feelings, and our feelings cause our moods to change. Your mood might change from happy in the morning to sad in the afternoon and then back to happy before bedtime. You might tell a friend, "I just don't feel like myself today," after fighting with a sibling. Negative emotions might keep you from feeling like your normal, happy self for a little bit. It might not always seem like it, but if you know what to do, you can handle your changing moods, no matter the size of the waves.

MY FEELINGS

Have you ever known a friend or classmate who got a new puppy? Maybe you were jealous at first but then felt happy for them. We can have so many different feelings in a short span of time, but the better you become at identifying your feelings, the more prepared you will be to navigate your boat! Circle any feelings you've had today or in the past few days:

Confident	Annoyed	Relaxed
Serious	Stressed	Brave
Frustrated	Respectful	Moody
Kind	Calm	Silly
Joyful	Jealous	Anxious
Sad	Happy	Grumpy
Loving	Curious	Embarrassed
Excited	Impulsive	Fearful
Confused	Angry	Proud
Hopeful	Strong	Worried

Expressing Emotions

It's important to feel like you can be yourself, even when you're having strong emotions. If you didn't get to wear your favorite outfit for picture day, you might feel disappointed, and your mood may shift from happy to sad. You may be less talkative when you're upset or want to be left alone. When this happens, your friends may comment or ask what's wrong. This means that you've expressed yourself in a way that tells others a story about how you feel. Emotional expression is the way you choose to show your feelings. There is no wrong or right way to do this, but some ways of expressing your emotions are healthier than others.

Brain Talk

There are five main parts of the brain that help shape our emotions and actions. Let's call them the brain's VIPs (Very Important Parts). Four of the VIPs are the **amygdala**, **hippocampus**, **thalamus**, and **hypothalamus**. They help shape the way we act and feel, and they make up our **limbic system**, the fifth VIP. The limbic system is an area of the brain that manages most of our emotions, feelings, and moods. Although these VIPs have different responsibilities, they come together to do one important job: keep us safe, alert, and healthy. You know when your teacher asks you to sit quietly throughout the day so class will run smoothly? These VIPs kind of do the same for your brain.

Amygdala (uh-mig-duh-luh) This is a small but mighty part of your brain. Think of the amygdala as the engine of your boat. It manages many of your emotions—especially fear. Fear is a helpful emotion that keeps us safe from harm. If your amygdala senses harm, your body will produce hormones to help keep you safe. You may notice sweaty hands or a faster heartbeat. This "fight, flight, or freeze" response can help you protect yourself in dangerous situations.

Hypothalamus (hy-poh-thal-uh-mus) Have you ever felt grumpy at school because you couldn't sleep the night before? This brain structure really wants you to get enough sleep so you're in a good mood the next day. The hypothalamus helps create a sleep pattern

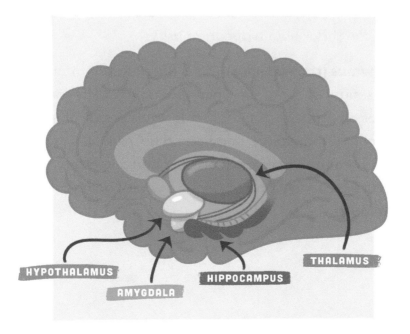

that your body is used to. It also helps you notice when you're hungry, thirsty, too hot, or too cold. All of these things can change your mood!

Hippocampus (hip-poh-camp-us) This one sounds like an African animal, but it's a super-cool part of your brain! Have you ever driven by a friend's old house after they moved and instantly felt sad? The hippocampus helps your brain with memory by connecting it with an emotion and sometimes even a smell. Maybe your younger brother is starting kindergarten in your old classroom, and the smell of that room brings back memories from when you were his age. This is your hippocampus at work. Speaking of the classroom, this part of the brain helps you remember what you've read and learned. If you remember some things from this book, you can thank your hippocampus!

Thalamus (thal-uh-mus) This is the great emotional messenger of our brain. Once your amygdala experiences an emotion, the thalamus sends signals through your brain to help you understand it. Think of it as a mailroom that receives a ton of important letters telling us how to feel and respond to what's going on around us.

Levels of Feelings

All our feelings come from basic or "primary" emotions. The six primary emotions are happiness, sadness, anger, fear, disgust, and surprise. These primary emotions are what you notice first, right after something has happened. Then you might start to feel "secondary" emotions. If you get a bad grade on a test, your primary emotion might be sadness and your secondary might be worry, when you think about what your parents will say.

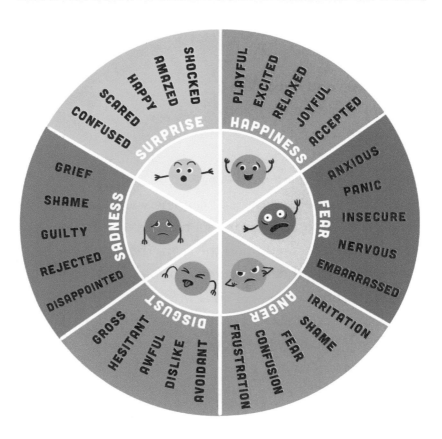

Helpful Hormones

Hormones are chemicals that our brain sends to different parts of our body so change and growth can happen. Hormones can also help you feel ready to run when you're scared, happy when you hug your parent, proud of yourself when you do well at school, or embarrassed when someone makes fun of you. Let's explore:

Oxytocin (oxy-tos-in) Scientists call this the love hormone because it helps us feel and express love. This hormone helps us feel safe, secure, and less anxious. When you hug your best friend, your body releases oxytocin. This explains why it feels so good to love and be loved in return!

Serotonin and dopamine (ser-uh-ton-in), (doh-puh-meen) These are our happy hormones. Have you ever made an A on a test and felt proud of yourself? Well, this is because your hard work paid off and your body released dopamine to reward you. The more accomplished you feel, the more dopamine your brain is making. Serotonin is what your body releases when you play outside or run around the gym. The more you exercise your body, the more serotonin your body makes and the better you feel. This is why exercise is good for your mood. If you don't have enough dopamine or serotonin, you may feel moody or sad or have trouble paying attention.

Adrenaline and cortisol (uh-dren-ah-lin), (cor-ti-sol)

Think of these hormones as your defenders. Remember the "fight, flight, or freeze" response we talked about? Adrenaline and cortisol help keep you safe from harm by preparing your body to run, fight back, or freeze in place. These hormones can be helpful or harmful. If you're on a road trip with your family and another car almost hits you, these hormones will help your parent react fast so everyone in the car can stay safe. But these hormones can be harmful when your body thinks it's in trouble when it's not. Like if your body tells you you're in danger because you failed a quiz at school, it will make these hormones even though they aren't very helpful in that situation. It's a wonderful thing that your body is trying to keep you safe from harm, but it's important to know when you are or aren't in actual danger. The next section will show you some of the ways you can handle your emotions in these types of situations.

MY EMOTIONAL SCORE

How well do you understand emotions? Take this quiz to find out! Read the statement, and then decide how well it describes you.

1. When I am feeling angry or frustrated, I know that these are normal emotions that will go away soon.

   a. Yes, most of the time
   b. Sometimes
   c. No, not usually

2. I show my friends I care about them by asking them how they're feeling.

   a. Yes, most of the time
   b. Sometimes
   c. No, not usually

3. I know that my mood can affect others around me and that their mood can affect me, too.

   a. Yes, most of the time
   b. Sometimes
   c. No, not usually

4. I try to be kind and cheerful to my friends, even when I am feeling grumpy or sad.

   a. Yes, most of the time

b. Sometimes

c. No, not usually

5. When I feel sad or think I might cry, I talk to a trusted grown-up or friend instead of keeping it bottled up inside.

a. Yes, most of the time

b. Sometimes

c. No, not usually

6. I'm a good listener when my friends are having a bad day, because I know what it's like to have a bad day, too.

a. Yes, most of the time

b. Sometimes

c. No, not usually

7. I know that emotions are a normal part of being human and everyone feels and expresses them differently.

a. Yes, most of the time

b. Sometimes

c. No, not really

8. When I am confused about my feelings, I talk about them with a trusted grown-up.

a. Yes, most of the time

b. Sometimes

c. No, not usually

Give yourself 3 points for every a, 2 points for every b, and 1 point for every c.

Did you score an 18 or above? Woohoo! You're off to a great start navigating your changing feelings and emotions. Keep reading this book to learn even more about yourself.

If you scored under 18, don't worry! We're all learning together, and you should feel proud of what you already know. Congratulate yourself for answering honestly, and keep reading for lots of advice and activities that will help you learn so much more.

HOW CAN I FEEL BETTER?

We all have emotions—lots of them. But it's important to know how to deal with them in a way that leaves you feeling better, not worse. There are no right or wrong emotions to have, but there are some not-so-nice ways of expressing yourself, such as fighting or yelling. I'm going to share some tips and tricks for handling your emotions. They can help you feel better when you feel bad and can help you express yourself in the healthiest way. When you're able to express yourself in a calmer or kinder manner, your friendships and relationships with others are better, too. Let's talk about some of these techniques:

Breathe deeply.

Thankfully, breathing is so automatic that we never have to think about doing it! Sometimes, though, it can be helpful to notice your breaths and practice breathing deeply and slowly. Deep breathing lowers your feelings of anxiety and can make you feel

calm and even sleepy. There are a couple of fun ways to practice deep breathing:

Take a big, deep breath in for four seconds, hold it for another four seconds, and then slowly exhale for another four seconds. Repeat this a few times until you feel calm.

Place your favorite stuffed animal or blanket on your tummy and watch it go up and down as you take big, deep breaths in and out.

Relax those muscles.

When we feel stressed out, our brain sends a message to the body to prepare for danger. This causes our muscles to feel tense. If this happens a lot, it can cause pain throughout your body, such as headaches or sore shoulders. To relax your tight muscles, try this:

Take a big breath in, and squeeze those muscles until they feel tight or tense. Then relax and slowly let go of the pressure, breathing out as you go. For example, try putting both of your fists into a tight ball and holding it for a few seconds before letting go slowly. When you let go, breathe out slowly and count to 10. It's helpful to relax your shoulders and jaw as you release, too.

Exercise it out.

Exercise is great for your mind *and* body. Here's how to get some happy hormones going inside you:

Next time you're feeling angry or sluggish, or just looking for something to do, turn to your favorite exercise: run, dance, bike, whatever! Ask a parent to take you to dance, karate, or swim practice for an extra dose of these hormones. Grab a friend or sibling and jump rope, walk, toss a ball, or hula-hoop—it all counts.

Sleep tight.

Did you know your body does important work while you sleep? If you sleep less than nine hours, your body probably didn't get to do all its work, so you may feel grumpy or sleepy. You may feel too tired in class to answer questions, which could leave you feeling disappointed in yourself. Here are a few ways to make sure you're getting good sleep at night:

- ◆ Go to bed around the same time each night.
- ◆ Avoid sugary drinks before bed.
- ◆ Try not to eat dinner right before bed.
- ◆ Turn off electronics an hour before bedtime.
- ◆ Read a book or listen to calming music or sounds.

Find your safe space.

Close your eyes and let your imagination take over! I want you to imagine and describe your happiest or safest place. This can be a real place you've been, or you can make it up and decorate it how you want. Be sure to include:

- ◆ The sights, including the color of the walls or sky
- ◆ The smells
- ◆ The temperature
- ◆ The sounds
- ◆ What you're wearing
- ◆ Who is or isn't there

Be as detailed and creative as you want—you may even want to imagine what superpowers you have!

Want to relax even more? Do this activity along with deep breathing.

MY FAVORITE THINGS

Good memories can always make us smile. Did you know that one way to handle difficult emotions is to look back on your favorite memories? These memories might be from when you laughed so hard with a friend that you both couldn't talk or a favorite vacation. Scrapbooking is a fun way to put all those memories in one special place.

To get started, visit your nearest crafts store or "go shopping" in your house with materials you already own. You may want to use scrapbook or construction paper, markers, pens, colored pencils, stickers, stamps, favorite photos you are allowed to cut and glue, safe scissors, glue, stencils, or anything else that makes you happy.

Start by setting aside a page for each of your favorite memories. Now get creative and fill the scrapbook with your most special memories. You can turn to it whenever you're feeling down.

Practice mindfulness.

Do you ever feel that your thoughts and feelings are like a loud storm in your head? Sometimes you may wish you could quiet that storm. You can, and here's how:

Try to imagine your thoughts or feelings as clouds passing by in the sky. When you watch the clouds, you simply notice and appreciate them for what they are. You can do this with your thoughts, too! Try "sitting with them," imagining them as clouds passing by or labeling them with feeling words.

For example, you could say to yourself, "I know I am feeling sadness. I am going to sit with it until it goes by on its own because I know it will." Mindfulness doesn't make your thoughts or feelings go away, but it helps you accept them and enjoy the present moment, instead of worrying about the past or the future.

Here's another mindfulness trick: Slowly draw your name in fun letters on a piece of paper. Pay attention to each stroke of the marker, noticing the shapes you're creating, while also paying attention to your thoughts and feelings as you go along.

Find ways to practice self-care.

Self-care is exactly what it sounds like—taking care of yourself! Here's a self-care exercise that can help you feel good about yourself:

Start by making two lists. Create one list with some of your favorite activities. It could be taking a bath, going to the movies, or eating pizza. Make a second list with some activities that you don't always want to do but know you'd feel proud of afterward, like doing a chore or getting started on a school project.

Notice how both lists help you take care of yourself—sometimes in a fun way, other times in a way that will help your future self. Self-care sets you up to feel good tomorrow, next week, and next year.

Now combine each list and do one or a few self-care activities every day. Mix it up—do things from both lists. Self-care activities, whether practicing your favorite sport or raking the leaves in the yard, help you feel better because you are having fun and relaxing while still taking care of your needs and responsibilities.

Use good body language.

Body language is the way we hold our shoulders, the volume of our voice, the way we move our hands, and our eye contact and facial expressions. It tells others a lot about us and how we're feeling. Do you slump your shoul-  ders when someone picks on you? Do you sit up straight and shoot up your hand when you know an answer? As you can see, body language can be positive or negative, but positive body language makes us feel better and more confident! Here are two ways to help you become aware of body language and use it to change how you feel:

Stand in front of a mirror. Practice how you might appear if you were scared, or embarrassed, or proud. Notice how your face and posture and body show your feelings. How can you change these to be more positive?

Practice confident body language. Try standing up straight, speaking up clearly, or doing a superhero pose in front of the mirror. And when you feel negative body lan-guage coming on, use these tricks to stand proud!

Talk it out.

Feelings can be overwhelming! Talking to a friend, family member, or trusted grown-up is a great way to make sense of your feelings. When you are upset, or even experiencing several different emotions, you might feel confused and stressed.

Talking to someone you trust can help you figure out why you're feeling those emotions. More importantly, talking things through can make you feel better and not so alone.

The next time you feel stressed, seek out a trusted grown-up to talk to. You may not want to immediately talk about what's bothering you, and that's okay. Just spending time with someone who cares about you can help you feel better and more relaxed, and you may soon feel comfortable enough to open up to them.

Who Is a "Trusted Grown-up"?

Talking to your friends about your feelings is okay and can be helpful at times, but a trusted grown-up might be able to help more because they have already experienced many of the same feelings you're having, and they can give you advice and support. A trusted grown-up is someone you feel comfortable and safe around. They want you to feel happy and would never hurt you physically or emotionally. They will not ask you to keep secrets from other adults or to do or say anything you aren't comfortable with. This might be a parent, school counselor, teacher, coach, or grandparent.

Not everyone is a trusted grown-up. Always remember, if you get a weird gut feeling when talking to someone, pay attention to this feeling, because this person might not be what you consider a trusted grown-up.

When you want to talk to a trusted grown-up, start by telling them how you're feeling. For example, you can say, "I'm sad that my friends left me out, and I want to talk about it when you have time."

The more you practice turning to a trusted grown-up in your life, the more confident you'll become talking about your feelings!

I KNOW WHAT TO DO!

You just learned all kinds of tricks for handling your emotions—now see if you can connect each situation below with a good trick to deal with it. Happy matching!

Feeling jealous of the new girl

Find a safe space

Feeling angry at your best friend for spending more time with another friend

Do some deep breathing

Feeling anxious in the car or on a road trip with your family

Exercise mindfulness

Feeling embarrassed after missing the ball during a softball game

Practice self-care

Feeling proud after getting a good grade on your math quiz

Change your body language

Feeling disappointed that your mom or dad couldn't chaperone the field trip

Exercise

Feeling sad or unmotivated to do your favorite things

Talk it out

Did you find good tricks for each situation? Everyone is different, and there is no wrong answer. Each of these tricks can be helpful for any situation.

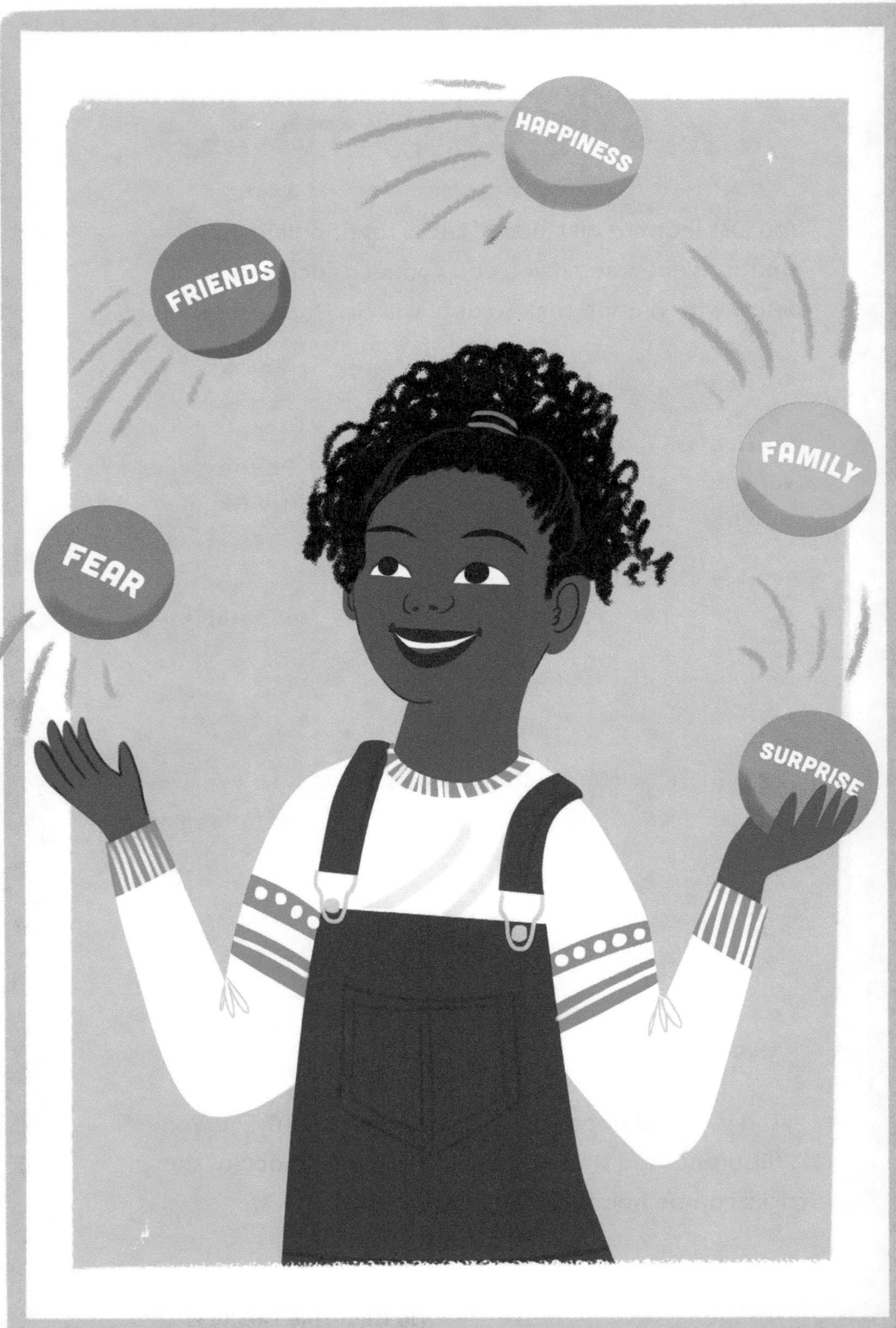
HAPPINESS
FRIENDS
FAMILY
FEAR
SURPRISE

MY CHANGING MIND

Now you know that every single day, you're growing and changing. Hopefully, you're also realizing you can think harder, juggle more responsibilities, and be yourself with your friends and family. Would you have thought five years ago that one day you'd be able to make your own lunch, play a sport, get good grades, and be a good friend, all at the same time? That's the exciting part of growth and change. Some changes you go through can be unexpected, but everyone goes through them, and guess what? There is no right or wrong way to feel. As these changes happen, if you can learn to manage your emotions in a positive way, it will leave you feeling empowered—like you can handle anything!

A POSITIVE MINDSET

All of these changing emotions can be confusing! You may notice that your emotions feel stronger when you're hungry or tired, or when you get bad news. It's true that our emotions affect how we feel, think, and act, but it's important to know that they don't make us who we are. We are separate from our emotions, just like we are separate from our mistakes. You can make a mistake and still be a good person, just like you can feel sad but still be your happy, joyful self at the end of the day. The best way to do this is to notice your changing emotions, deal with them, but remain the awesome person you are.

Even if you are a positive person, you may experience a negative emotion or have a bad day, and it might feel like you're never going to get back to that happy, bubbly personality of yours. Thankfully, this isn't true! Positive and negative emotions come and go, but it's how you act when you feel them that matters.

Positive emotions can cause positive actions, while negative emotions can cause negative actions. Sometimes, when we're experiencing a tough emotion, we accidentally do things that make us feel worse, like yell at someone we care about. In between this feeling and action, there is usually a thought. This thought is your inner voice! Your inner voice helps you decide if you're going to make a healthy decision, like to talk calmly, or an unhealthy one, like to yell.

Let's think of your negative and positive thoughts as colors, like **RED** and **GREEN**.

A negative inner voice, or red thought, might sound like, "No one asked me to join their group in art today. It's probably because I'm bad at painting. I'm just going to quit trying." A positive inner voice, or green thought, might sound like, "I was able to paint alone today, and I paint really well when I'm not distracted. I am proud of myself, but tomorrow I'd like to ask my friends if they want to work together."

Your inner voice is powerful, and it might feel impossible to stop the red thoughts, but with a little practice, you can change your negative mindset by turning your red thoughts into green ones. Here's how:

1. Notice the negative thought.
2. Challenge yourself to find something good in the situation.
3. Reword the thought so it focuses on the good things instead of the bad.

Here are some examples of turning red thoughts into green ones:

RED THOUGHT: My best friend didn't sit next to me at lunch today. She must not like me anymore.

GREEN THOUGHT: My best friend chose to sit next to a new friend today, and I know it has nothing to do with how she feels about me. I'm proud of her because I know that's hard. There will be a day when I do that, too. I'd like to be the kind of friend who is accepting of my friends' decisions.

RED THOUGHT: I go to a separate classroom to get more help with reading. I must not be as smart as my classmates.

GREEN THOUGHT: I get the chance to go to a new classroom and have fun one-on-one time with my reading teacher. There are no distractions in there, and I've already learned a ton.

Another helpful way of quieting your red thoughts would be to label them and say, "Hey, I know this is a red thought, and my red thoughts usually aren't true. Hmm, let me think of a green thought on that subject!"

POSITIVE SELF-TALK

Complete a green thought by thinking about the positive in the situation instead of the negative.

RED: Charlie made fun of me for not spending the night away from home yet. She probably thinks I'm a baby.

GREEN: _____

_____

_____

RED: I heard my parents arguing last night about me and my brother. Is it our fault that they fight?

GREEN: _____

_____

_____

RED: I became angry at my teammate during soccer practice because she didn't do what she was supposed to. She probably won't speak to me now.

GREEN: _____

_____

_____

Fill in your own red and green thoughts for the last three:

RED: _____

_____

_____

GREEN: _____

_____

_____

RED: _____

_____

_____

GREEN: _____

_____

_____

RED: _____

_____

_____

GREEN: _____

_____

_____

FROM SELF-CONSCIOUS TO CONFIDENT

Do you ever feel like your classmates are watching everything you say and do? Maybe you tried to wear your clothes from last year and realized you've grown out of them. These are self-conscious thoughts and feelings, and they're super common in kids your age. Feeling self-conscious simply means you're very aware of yourself, and that is not always a bad thing. It can help you be thoughtful about your words and actions. You should give yourself a high-five for being so in tune with yourself! But too much self-consciousness can be negative and make you feel like you're not good enough.

Confidence is when you trust yourself and feel proud of your skills and who you are. Confidence can take time to grow, because it comes from trying new things, facing your fears, and getting lots of practice. Maybe you remember feeling proud of yourself after scoring a goal at your soccer game. This helped build your confidence because it showed you what you're capable of.

But you don't always have to be "good" at things to feel confident. If you know you worked hard, practiced, and tried your best, your confidence is also growing, and that's exciting. You can even grow your confidence by loving and accepting yourself for who you are and not worrying about what others think of you.

Want to trade self-consciousness for confidence? Try these tips:

- ♦ **If you're feeling self-conscious about your looks, try standing in front of the mirror in a strong, proud pose and say three things you love about yourself out loud. They can be about anything! Just focus on being you and not on what you think others think of you.**
- ♦ **If you're feeling self-conscious about participating in an activity or exercising in PE, try practicing some of these exercises at home with family or friends, such as going for a run. Sometimes, practicing things that you're worried about will help give you the confidence to do them later.**

Once you've done these activities, try writing what you liked about them in a journal so you can look back and feel proud of yourself for your progress.

Media Messages

Have you ever looked in the mirror and wished you looked different in some way? Body image is the way we view ourselves and feel about our body. We are so lucky to have the bodies that we do, no matter the shape, size, or ability, but sometimes it's easy to forget this!

You can see up to 600 images a day all around you. Computers, TVs, billboards, and magazines display these images, which all send a message, but these messages aren't always true or helpful.

It's important to know which messages are useful and truthful and which ones are untrue or negative. Be cautious of negative messages that try to influence your thoughts or the way you feel about yourself. Nobody is perfect. Even actresses and models have photographers or a team of makeup artists and hairstylists to primp and polish them. This isn't what they look like naturally!

The more you accept and love your body, the more confident you'll feel. One way to start loving your body more is to remind yourself that you are beautiful and unique. Say it out loud, into the mirror!

FROM EMBARRASSED TO COMFORTABLE

Have you ever been embarrassed? I know I have! If you've ever noticed your face turn red or felt like you wanted to hide from everyone, that's embarrassment. It can be caused by anything that makes you feel silly or worry about what others think of you. Maybe you mispronounced a word while reading aloud in class, or you tripped and everyone saw. Embarrassment happens, and it's perfectly normal.

Embarrassment can stick with you and feel like it's never going to go away. It's important to know that it *will* go away, and you're not the only one feeling like this. Whenever you're feeling embarrassed, try to remember all the wonderful things that make you special. And remember, when a classmate does something embarrassing, you don't think about it all day, so they probably don't think about something you did, either!

Although it's not nice to laugh at others, it's definitely good to learn how to laugh at yourself. By learning to laugh at yourself with friends and family, you can turn embarrassment into confidence. Each time you feel embarrassed, think of it as a small step on a ladder toward self-confidence. As you learn to be comfortable laughing at yourself, trust that you're growing into the best person you want to be.

FROM SHY TO BRAVE

You might know a friend or a classmate who has always been very quiet. Maybe others call this person "snobby," "bratty," or "too quiet." But some people are just shy and keep to themselves—and that's totally okay. Shyness is a feeling of being uncomfort-able speaking up or talking in front of others. Kids who are shy feel more comfortable keeping quiet or staying in the background so that they aren't noticed or looked at.

Sometimes shyness is a natural part of someone's personality, but sometimes it comes from a worry of not being accepted. If you've ever been the new kid at school, you know it can be hard to open up and begin making new friends. This is a good example of how being shy feels. Kids who feel shy want friends just like other kids do, but they feel less comfortable joining in.

Being shy can make someone feel lonelier than they want to. If you are shy, there are things you can do to give yourself the courage to speak up.

One way is to begin writing down things you can say in group settings or with a new friend. When a group of friends is doing an activity that you're interested in, you could say, "Hi, my name is _____! Mind if I join?"

Another good way to build courage is to ask another kid about themselves. This can be easier if they are a new kid or seem to be shy or alone also. You could ask them their name, their favorite sport, or how they did on the math test. With practice, you'll soon have the courage to ask if they want to hang out sometime!

Remember that being shy and keeping to yourself on the playground isn't the same as being careful around strangers. Only talk to adults who you know are trusted grown-ups. If you're scared to speak up in class or on the playground, then you might be experiencing shyness. If you're cautious around a stranger who is trying to talk to you, then you're being smart and safe.

FROM ANXIOUS TO CALM

Anxiety is a feeling that comes from fear. Fear is a "primary" emotion we have, like sadness, happiness, and anger. Fear and anxiety can be helpful emotions. They can help keep us safe when our body and mind decide that we're in danger.

Sometimes our brain makes us think we're in danger even when we're not. It does this to help keep us safe, but too much of it can cause us to feel worried all the time. Too much worry can cause you to feel tired, and it can take up space in your mind that should hold fun, positive thoughts instead.

You may feel anxious around big dogs, before sports team tryouts, or when you walk into school. There are different types of anxiety, and all of them are normal every now and then. If you're scared of spiders, big dogs, or getting shots at the doctor, then you might have a phobia or fear of these things. If you feel anxious about leaving your mom or dad or staying the night at a friend's house, then you might have separation anxiety. If you're worried about a big exam or being liked by your friends, then you might be experiencing some general anxiety. These are all common. Usually, using the tricks we talked about on pages 13 to 21 will help, such as mindfulness, exercise, or self-care. While certain fears can be normal, they are no fun to live with every day. If any of these types of anxiety become too hard to deal with, tell a trusted grown-up or your school counselor.

FROM ANGRY TO PEACEFUL

Anger can be a tough emotion to deal with, because we don't feel totally ourselves when we're angry. Anger is only a feeling. It is not who we are. When we're angry, our brain is so busy trying to make sense of what we're angry about that it doesn't let us think straight. When we're able to think clearly, we make better decisions and we're usually kinder to others.

Has your brother or sister ever blamed you for something they did? Maybe you got even with them, and then you were the one who got into trouble. There are better ways to deal with anger. Counting to 10, going to your imaginary "safe space," or writing down what you want to say to them can all help you think clearly before acting.

Maybe when you're angry, you like to scream into a pillow or squeeze your fists into a tight ball. Maybe your friend likes to stay quiet and prefers no one talk to her until she feels better. No matter how you act, it is okay, as long as you aren't hurting anyone else or yourself.

Bullying

No one likes being bullied, and no one deserves it, either.

Bullying is a common but often painful issue that can cause deep feelings of anger, helplessness, and isolation. But bullying itself can sometimes be a result of anger, frustration, jealousy, or sadness. Have you felt any of these emotions and hurt a friend or sibling but then felt bad about it afterward? Not dealing with your feelings in a healthy way can sometimes lead to bullying, whether you mean it or not. Dealing with your emotions in a healthy way, like doing deep breathing or talking things out, can help keep you from hurting someone else whenever you're hurting.

There are different ways to tell if you're getting bullied. If someone constantly picks on you, makes you feel bad, or leaves you feeling scared or anxious or like you don't want to go to school, then you might be getting bullied. Bullying can happen in person as well as online.

continued >

If you think you're being bullied:

1. Tell a trusted grown-up or mentor right away. Tell more than one grown-up if you need to.
2. Do what you can to avoid the person who's bullying you.
3. Stick with a friend.
4. Tell the teacher if the bully is in your class.
5. Change up your body language to appear more confident. Practice your superhero pose in the mirror while saying phrases like "Leave me alone" in a strong and powerful voice. You can say it to the bully when you feel safe and ready.
6. Don't keep it inside! Talk about it with those you trust.

Additionally, if the bullying happens online:

1. Don't respond.
2. Save the post.
3. Share it with a trusted grown-up. Together, find out your school's policy on online bullying and report it if you can.
4. Make sure your settings are private and block that individual.
5. Leave the scene—take a break from social media for a while.

FROM SAD TO HOPEFUL

Sadness is another one of our "primary" emotions, like happiness and anger. Whenever our body and mind experience a "primary" emotion, we notice them quickly because they often feel a lot stronger than other emotions. Sadness is a tough feeling, but it's also a natural and healthy emotion to have every now and then.

There are many different reasons we may feel sad. We can't tell our brain when to feel sad or not feel sad—it just happens! But we can choose to deal with it in the best possible way. Things that help fight off sadness might include playing music; dancing; drawing; doing a favorite sport, activity, or hobby; talking to a good friend; or standing in front of a mirror and saying positive things.

Grief is a type of sadness that sits in your mind after you've experienced a loss, like when someone you loved has passed away. Maybe a relative or pet recently died, and you've noticed more feelings of sadness or even anger. Grief can feel really strong and make you want to cry. Other times, you'll be able to go about your day, laughing and playing with friends. Grief can stick around or come and go. It is just a strong type of sadness that reminds us of how special that person (or pet) was to us and how much we will always love and remember them.

To help yourself deal with these feelings, try drawing or painting your grief. What does it "look like" to you? Maybe it's a dark rain cloud or a big scribble with lots of dark colors. Maybe there are bright colors in there, too, as you think about that person. Talking about your feelings and noticing how your grief and sadness feel in your body can help, too. Maybe one day you want to cry and another day your stomach aches or you aren't hungry—these are all normal signs of grief and sadness. Whether it's from losing a loved one or dealing with a situation at school, sadness is an important feeling that we all have, and it's a healthy one. However, if you feel strong sadness every day for most of the day, it's a good idea to tell a trusted grown-up like your parent, school counselor, or family doctor.

FROM JEALOUS TO GRATEFUL

Has your sibling or friend ever received more attention than you? Maybe they won a contest, or did a solo in the concert, or scored the game-winning goal. Maybe they were sick and everyone was fussing over them. You may think they're more important than you in that moment. You may start to compare yourself to them.

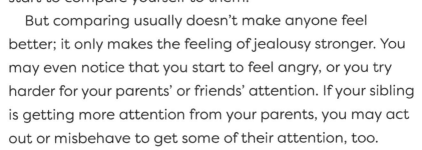

But comparing usually doesn't make anyone feel better; it only makes the feeling of jealousy stronger. You may even notice that you start to feel angry, or you try harder for your parents' or friends' attention. If your sibling is getting more attention from your parents, you may act out or misbehave to get some of their attention, too.

Jealousy is like pulling a dark curtain over your own special qualities, so you can't see them in the moment. When you're feeling this way, remind yourself what makes you special and unique. Do an activity that you know you're good at. While doing this activity, practice mindfulness and pay attention to your creativity.

You may notice that someone else is feeling jealous toward you and you don't know how to handle it, like a brother or sister during your birthday party. Maybe they don't understand why you're receiving special attention, and they're acting out. Remember to be kind and patient with them.

Feeling jealous does not make you a bad person. Ask yourself, "Why am I feeling like this, and what can I do to accept it and deal with it in a healthy way?" Maybe you can put yourself in the other person's shoes and consider how they would feel. How would you want to be treated if you were them?

Catch yourself if you start to compare yourself to others. You could say to yourself, "I think I'm feeling jealous. Let me think of things I am thankful for instead of things I am jealous of."

FEELING GRATEFUL

We all have things in our lives that make us happy, thankful, and grateful. But sometimes we can lose sight of what they are.

To practice gratitude, get a notebook or a few sheets of paper. Write the day of the week and something that makes you feel grateful today. This can be anything at all! If you're having trouble, try thinking about your day or looking around the room for things you're happy to see. This can be the macaroni and cheese on your lunch tray, the new friend next to you, your soccer ball, or the shoes on your feet.

Congratulations! You just started a gratitude journal. This helps you remember what's special and important in your life. You can write a grateful message daily and look at it when you're having a bad day. Just open your journal and remind yourself of all the things that make you feel your happiest.

HELP ANDY FEEL BETTER

You've learned so much! Now choose the best advice to give your friend Andy, who might be experiencing similar feelings:

1. **Andy is afraid of presenting in front of the class tomorrow. It makes her feel very nervous. You:**

   a. Tell another friend and laugh together at Andy.

   b. Tell Andy you're nervous, too, and remind her that you will be there for her after the presentation to talk if she wants to.

   c. Make Andy feel silly for being nervous by saying, "Give me a break—you need to get a grip."

   Answer: B *Reminding Andy that she is not the only one who is feeling nervous is a good way to connect with your friend and remind each other that these emotions are perfectly normal. Offering support and a listening ear is a great way to be there for a friend, and it will show her that she can be there for you in this way one day, too.*

2. Andy keeps following you around at a party because she is feeling shy. You:

   a. Try to shake her off by hiding in a bathroom.
   b. Introduce Andy to people you know and tell them something they have in common, like, "Hey, aren't you both in the school choir?" Encourage her to join you in activities.
   c. Tell Andy she needs to back off because it is annoying you.

   Answer: B *Helping someone who is shy get out of their comfort zone is kind and a great way to build your own confidence. It's also fun to do this together, because you're making new friends and memories at the same time.*

3. You heard that Andy said something untrue about you to other friends. You:

   a. Calmly ask her if she can talk later and set aside a time for you, her, and maybe even a trusted grown-up to talk out the problem. Maybe this is a misunderstanding or not even true.
   b. Start saying mean things about her to your other friends.
   c. Tell her you're no longer going to be friends.

Answer: A *Talking problems out is a helpful way to solve a problem without causing more problems in the meantime. If needed, a trusted grown-up can offer advice and keep the conversation from getting too mean or angry.*

4. A classmate is picking on Andy for being taller than the rest of the kids in the class. You:

   a. Join your classmate in making fun of Andy, because you did not like that Andy was taller than you.
   b. Tell her to pick on the classmate for being shorter than her.
   c. Suggest to Andy that she make a list of what she loves about herself. Remind her that everyone's body is different and she is beautiful just the way she is.

   Answer: C *Making a list of what she loves about herself will remind her what she's proud of and that everyone is unique and has awesome qualities. Your compliments will also help her feel good about herself.*

5. Andy comes to school angry because her parents made her apologize to her brother. She feels like she didn't do anything wrong. You:

a. Tell her, "Get over it. I just lost my homework."

b. Show her how to do deep breathing, and encourage her to wait until she is calm and ready to talk to her parents.

c. Tell her it's okay for her to be mad all day and treat others unkindly since she is angry.

Answer: B *You'll help Andy calm down by showing her deep breathing or whatever tricks work for you. This way, she won't hurt anyone else because of her anger, and she might have a better, happier day.*

6. **Andy tells you she's been having negative thoughts all day and doesn't know how to stop. You:**

a. Show her your trick for how to change a red thought to a green one (page 27) and see if she wants to practice it with you.

b. Tell her, "Don't worry. I'm sure they'll go away soon. It's no big deal."

c. Laugh at her negative thoughts when she shares them with you.

Answer: A *Now that you're a pro at turning red thoughts into green ones, show her your trick and let her know that it's totally normal to have red thoughts some days.*

7. Andy tells you that she thinks she's getting bullied on the playground, but she's not sure and is asking you for advice. You:

a. Ask her what the person is doing and suggest she talk to a trusted grown-up or teacher right away. Check in with her later and make sure she got the help she needed.

b. Tell her to confront the person on her own.

c. Laugh at her and say, "No one is a bully at our school. You'll be fine!"

Answer: A *By doing this, you're letting Andy know that you care about her safety, but you're also pointing her in the right direction to seek help from a trusted grown-up.*

MY BFF!

ME AND MOM

CRAZY DAD!!

SWEET MOLLY

MY CHANGING RELATIONSHIPS

You are changing, and you may also be noticing changes in your relationships with others. You might feel more sensitive when your teacher corrects you in class, or more self-conscious around friends. These changes are perfectly normal! Whether they happen with your family, a friend, or a classmate, there are healthy ways to handle them.

We all like being with people who treat us kindly, laugh with us instead of at us, and listen when we need to talk. Friends are the people in your life who know what you're going through and accept you no matter how happy and silly you choose to be.

But as you grow, you may feel uncertain about these friendships. You might even notice some friendships will change—sometimes because of fights, peer pressure, or even just new interests. While it can feel sad or confusing to drift away from a friend, you are not alone—this happens to almost everyone! I'll share some good tips to help you work through these changes and even see the bright side of things.

You may start to notice changes taking place at home, too. Maybe when you were younger, you talked to your family about everything, but now you feel self-conscious when your parents ask you questions. Maybe you think they won't understand, or you just want your privacy. This is all a part of growing up.

It can help to look at these changes as the beginning of growth and strength within yourself. Let's talk about different ways to handle these changes so you can stay true to your wonderful, strong self and still feel connected to the people you love.

FRIENDS

There are times when a trusted grown-up is the best person to talk to. But friends can offer a different, special kind of support. Friends have a unique way of relating to you, laughing with you, and listening to you. Have you and a friend ever made up a language or secret hand-shake? That's a way of communicating that only you and your friend have. These types of friendships are important because they keep things fun and not-so-serious!

But along with friendships come some serious things, like peer pressure, making new friends, ending friendships, and dealing with bullying and cliques (a tight circle of friends). We all make new friends and end old friendships throughout our life, and that's normal. No one does this perfectly, but let's talk about some of the best ways to handle these issues.

Making New Friends

Do you remember when you made your very first friend? You might not if you were very little. Humans have a natural ability to make friends even at a young age, because somehow, our body and mind know that healthy friendships keep us happy! There's always room for new friends, no matter how many you already have. But making friends can sometimes feel scary, right? You may worry that no one will accept you, or you might get frustrated when you feel left out.

Guess what? You already know some tricks to use to make yourself feel better when you're nervous about making new friends. Try changing up your body language, relaxing, or turning your negative thoughts into positive ones. You wouldn't want a negative thought to trick you out of becoming friends with your future best friend, would you? Remember, fear and worry can be helpful, but they can fool us sometimes.

I trust that you're going to make new friends in no time, but here are a few tips to help you make those connections:

- ◆ Try to be kind.
- ◆ Show interest in others.
- ◆ Ask friends questions about themselves.
- ◆ Be a good listener.
- ◆ Give compliments.
- ◆ Make plans to hang out outside of school, not just in class.

If you feel nervous when trying these, that's a good sign. It means you are brave and growing.

Every day is a chance to make a new friend or learn from someone new. It might be hard to imagine right now, but you will have all kinds of friends come and go and some will be a better fit for you than others.

Making new friends doesn't mean you have to forget about your old friends, either. You can bring your old and new friends together by introducing them to one another to form one big, fun group. You could say to a new friend, "I have a friend that I've known for a few years. I think you'll like her, too. Do you want to meet her sometime?"

But don't settle for any friend, new or old, who has repeatedly hurt your feelings or isn't kind to you. Sometimes it's time to step away from a friendship if it doesn't feel good anymore. There's no need to fight or be unkind—just give the relationship a little space. Maybe it will work out and you'll be friends again, and maybe it won't, but it's important to choose to be around people who make you feel good about yourself and whom you can have fun with.

Cliques

As you make new friends, you may notice you all grow into one big group of friends that do everything together. Or maybe you prefer to hang out with one or two of your closest friends in a smaller setting.

No matter what you prefer, you will likely be a part of a group at some point in life. There are many different types and sizes of groups out there. Small groups, large groups, sports groups, church groups, groups that do arts and crafts. You can start your own group and invite anyone who wants to join, like a dog-walking or scrap-booking group. Maybe even a group where you teach your dog how to scrapbook! Just kidding—that might be a little difficult.

There are all kinds of personalities in groups, but that's the wonderful part about them. In a good group, everyone is included and invited, no matter what.

Cliques are a little different. A clique is a tight group of friends. This might be a group of kids who all play basketball or musical instruments, but it may also be a group of kids who just enjoy each other's company. These groups can feel like "your people" and give you a feeling of belonging. A good clique will never try to change who you are, make you feel left out, or make you feel bad about yourself.

Some cliques are not so positive. A bad clique may gossip or make silly rules that try to control you. In a clique, you might only be allowed to wear blue or have to sit in the same spot every day at lunch. People in these cliques might not be "allowed" to talk or hang out with anyone outside of the clique, which isn't very fun or nice. You might notice more peer pressure in cliques or feel like you can't be yourself.

If you are feeling controlled, left out, or bullied by someone in a clique, step away and know that there are plenty of groups and friends out there who would love for you to join them. If you need help finding a group to join, start by telling a friend or trusted grown-up what you're interested in and see if they can suggest the right group for you.

No matter if you're a part of a group or clique, try to remember others' feelings and always be inviting. These experiences begin to shape the person you are going to be for life. As the saying goes, "Whatever you are, be a good one."

Peer Pressure

As you grow older, you'll learn more about what you like or don't like, who you are or aren't, and what you're comfortable with. Sometimes this will be fun and easy, and other times it can be hard and confusing. The important thing to know is that you don't have to let anyone pressure you into doing something that doesn't feel right.

It's easy to stick up for yourself around people you aren't worried about, like family and old friends. But what about the people in your life whom you like and want to be liked by in return—like peers, classmates, and new friends? When we're worried about being liked, it can feel harder to say no or be independent. Saying no and making your own decisions doesn't make you bad or boring. It makes you strong and a leader. You already have the strength within you to stay true to your values and awesomeness— so let's practice how to do it!

When you're feeling pressured or having a hard time deciding what to do, make three lists on a sheet of paper, colored red, yellow, and green (or pick your favorite colors).

Let's pretend Jamie wants you to help him pick on the new kid.

Your **red list** has reasons not to do something, or the reasons you're feeling uncertain.

Examples: I don't want to be mean to someone; that would hurt their feelings.

The **yellow list** has reasons you're thinking about doing something—are you feeling pressured, or do you think it would be fun?

Examples: I want Jamie to like me; I don't want to be picked on myself.

The **green list**, your "personal list," has your special qualities, or reasons you feel proud of yourself. (You could name this list "my special qualities" or decorate your name at the top.)

Examples: I always try to be kind to others; I do what I want, not what others tell me to do.

Think about all three lists or share the lists with a trusted grown-up who can help you decide. Is it more important to look cool to a classmate who is pressuring you? Or is it more important to stay true to who you are?

Consent

Your feelings and body are your own and no one else's, and you have the right to privacy and comfort. Just like you might need permission to use the Internet or walk to a friend's house, others need permission to touch or talk to you in a certain way. When you give permission, you're **giving** consent.

Getting consent means getting permission from others, while considering their feelings and respecting their privacy and comfort. Some people don't want to be hugged or talked to in a certain way, and that's okay.

Consent isn't just for in-person conversations. It's also for anything online. You're allowed to ask others to not talk to you a certain way online if it makes you uncomfortable, just like you're allowed to do in person. If you take a group photo with friends, it is important to remember that not everyone shares their photos, so you need to ask for consent before posting it online. And in return, nobody has the right to share your photo or information online without your consent.

If you're uncomfortable and do not want to be touched or talked to, you have the right to say, "Please don't touch me." This type of statement doesn't make you rude. It reminds others to respect you. Practice these statements with a friend or a trusted grown-up, or in the mirror by yourself, so you feel comfortable using them in public.

If anyone makes you feel bad for asking for consent, they're probably not someone you want to be spending time with. Most importantly, if someone does something without your consent, no matter how small or big, please tell a trusted grown-up. That's what trusted grown-ups are for.

Social Media

Social media can be exciting and dangerous all at the same time. Social media can make us feel happy and allow us to connect with our friends by messaging them or posting goofy photos together. Maybe those friends live in another state or country, so it can be extra special to connect with them.

As fun and helpful as it can be, social media can also lead to drama, fights, or hurt feelings. If you see pictures of your friends doing fun things together, it can make you happy to see them, but it can also make you feel jealous or left out.

If you're noticing more negative feelings than positive ones, try taking a break from social media or ask your parents to help you spend less time on it. If you share your feelings about it with a trusted grown-up, they'll be able to help when you're feeling bad or unsafe when using it.

continued >

Also remember that anything you share on the Internet is always going to be out there. It doesn't go away, so you'll want to be careful and thoughtful about what you post or share with others.

It might feel cool or trendy to sign up for social media or download certain apps, but most social media platforms require you to be at least 13 years old before joining. These rules are designed to help keep you safe, happy, and healthy.

Here are few ways to make sure you're using social media safely:

♦ Make sure your profile is private so you can control who sees your posts.
♦ Ask a parent or trusted grown-up to help set your profile to private and block anyone who makes you feel uncomfortable.
♦ Never talk to strangers on the Internet, even if someone says they are a kid, looks like a real person, or says they know someone you know. A lot of people pretend on the Internet, and it can be hard to know who is telling the truth.

FAMILY

Families come in all shapes, sizes, and forms—big families, small families, families with stepparents, families with only a mom or dad, families with two moms or two dads, families formed by adoption, families who have experienced a loss, and many more. You may be close to your parents, or you may live with and be cared for by aunts, uncles, or grandparents. No matter the shape or form, your family's job is to support you, guide you, and stand by your side during whatever changes you're going through.

Roles and Responsibilities

Every family has its own pattern of relationships between family members and a different way that everyone acts around each other. This pattern will shift throughout life as you and your family members grow and change. Your mom or dad could be going through their own changes, like moving into a different house or getting a new job. Maybe you're the youngest in the family, and your siblings treat you like the "baby." As you grow older, you'll notice that you have more responsibilities, and you deserve to be treated like the young adult you're blossoming into. If a family member gets sick or has passed away, that can cause a shift, too. These shifts and changes can make your emotions feel stronger or harder to deal with.

Changes and shifts happen with every family. Treat your family members like co-captains of your boat and let them help you navigate the big and little waves.

Getting Along

Maybe everyone in your family—dog, cat, and fish—are all getting along great right now. If so, hooray! That's great news. But maybe you and your sibling are fighting more than you used to, or maybe your feelings are stronger than before, and you don't think anyone would understand. Even if you're worried that your family members wouldn't get it, they do care, and it can be helpful to share your thoughts and feelings with them.

Activities, conversation starters, and games are some easy ways to break the ice so you can communicate with each other a little more easily.

A fun conversation starter is a question that starts with an introduction, like "When you were my age . . .?" Take it from here by asking:

+ What was your favorite hobby?
+ Who was your best friend?
+ What subject were you terrible at?
+ Do you remember having strong emotions as a kid? Did you understand them?
+ Did you fight with your brothers?
+ Were you ever embarrassed (scared, pressured, etc.)?
+ What did you do for fun in the summer?
+ What food did you like? What food did you hate?

This is a fun way to find out what your parents were like when they were your age. You may learn a lot about them and discover they aren't so different from you!

While games and activities like these are fun and can help you grow closer, you might feel like you need your own space, and that's okay, too. If you're feeling this way, you can use "I" statements (we'll talk about these soon) and ask for some personal space. You could say, "I am feeling anxious and would like some privacy to relax and do my deep breathing. Can I please excuse myself?"

Boundaries

As you grow, it's natural to want more privacy or boundaries. Boundaries are all about respecting one another's privacy. You might want to run into your sister's room and borrow her favorite dress, but as she gets older, she asks you to please knock first. (She may not always say it this nicely, but she is asking you to respect her boundaries.)

This works both ways, and you have boundaries that others should respect, too. Wanting more privacy or having more boundaries doesn't mean you're rude or want to spend less time with someone. Your parents and older siblings were your age once, too, and they know how important boundaries are.

"I" STATEMENTS

"I" statements are honest messages that tell how you feel about something. They can help you say what you need and let others understand what you are feeling. And they all start with—you guessed it—"I." Here are some useful examples of "I" statements:

- ♦ "I feel anxious when you rush me in the mornings before school. Can we talk about things to do the night before so we aren't as rushed in the morning?"
- ♦ "I get mad when you don't look like you're listening. It hurts my feelings and makes me feel silly for talking. Would you please look at me?"
- ♦ "I feel embarrassed when you walk into my room. Can you please respect my privacy and knock first?"

Try it for yourself:

1. I feel _____

   when you _____

   _____

   _____

2. I feel _____

   when you _____

   _____

   _____

3. I feel _____

   when you _____

   _____

   _____

Asking for privacy, attention, and other things you need doesn't make you rude. It shows your maturity and growth. (You can even show your family this exercise so they understand where you're coming from!)

Love Yourself

It's normal to have all kinds of feelings at home, because we're usually more comfortable there than anywhere else. When we're comfortable, we tend to show our emotions a bit more. At home, you might feel anger, frustration, jealousy, and silliness all in one day. When you do:

♦ Remember that everyone has emotions, including everyone in your family. The important thing is that everyone respects feelings and each other and tries to listen.

♦ Find a safe place to try your helpful tricks, like mindfulness (page 18) or muscle relaxation (page 14).

♦ Talk it out with a trusted grown-up or friend.

♦ Write a list of what makes you special, unique, and strong.

♦ Express your feelings and get creative by drawing a family photo. If you're feeling mad at your family, draw your pets or friends instead.

ROLE MODELS AND MENTORS

Mentors are all around you. Think about your librarian, older sister, coach, or teacher. Many of these people act as mentors in your life simply by being themselves. Maybe your mentor is one of your family members or a friend's mom or dad. A mentor can be a parent figure, but they don't always have to be. Mentors want to see you grow and succeed, and they often listen well, give good advice, respect your boundaries, and have qualities you look up to. Think about the people in your life who care about you,

make things fun, and help you when you need it. If you want to learn more from that person, you can ask them if they can be your mentor. You could say, "I notice you help me with a lot, and I like learning from you. Could you act as my mentor?"

A positive role model is also someone you look up to and want to be more like. Positive role models have personality traits and qualities that you admire or that match up with your values or beliefs. Some of these qualities may be more obvious, like if they're smart or kind to others. Some may be less obvious, like if they're hard-working or humble. Unlike a mentor, a role model might not know you look up to them, because they could be a famous athlete, scientist, author, or politician whom you haven't met in person.

If you think you've found a positive role model or mentor, ask yourself what you like about them and make a list of the ways you want to be like them.

MY ROLE MODELS

Many qualities can make someone an awesome role model! Think about the people you admire and consider role models. Circle the qualities that describe them:

Kind   Knowledgeable   Brave

Positive   Funny   Accepting of others

Determined to do the right thing   Creative   Joyful

Honest   Determined   Emotionally strong

Not afraid to be themselves   Fun-loving   Caring toward others

Confident   A good communicator   A good listener

Understanding   Respectful   Humble

MY BEST SELF

Impressed with yourself yet? I am! You've done some extraordinary work to get here. You've learned about the connection between your body and mind, your hormones, feelings, emotions, and changing relationships. You've learned great tricks for handling your emotions and completed all kinds of quizzes and activities along the way. Give yourself a high-five and think about everything you've learned—you are clearly in charge of your boat and its course toward a promising future! I hope you feel empowered, fabulous, and proud of the strong, confident person you are.

FEELING EMPOWERED

Have you ever been to a buffet where you could pile all the pizza and dessert on your plate that you want, but you knew this decision wouldn't be the healthiest? So instead, you grabbed some veggies or a salad for a healthier balance. As you grow, you'll be faced with a buffet of choices in life, and you'll have the power and responsibility to select the healthiest choices for yourself. Your healthy choices might look different from a friend's or sibling's, and that doesn't mean yours or theirs are wrong. You can be different and healthy at the same time!

With your new knowledge and skills, you have the choice to make good decisions and take care of yourself and those you care about. Let's talk about some of the skills you've learned that you can choose to use:

+ You can manage strong emotions in ways that work best for you.
+ You can think more positively by turning red thoughts into green ones.
+ You can use good body language to feel and look more confident.
+ You can be kind toward others, and you can love and care for yourself.
+ You can help your friends learn the skills you have for managing strong emotions.

- You can accept ups and downs with friends and understand that your friends are going to go through their own changes, too.
- You can take steps to make new friends or identify and leave an unhealthy friendship.
- You can choose friends, groups, and cliques that work for you.
- You can respond to peer pressure and stay true to who you are and what you believe in.
- You can tell what makes a trusted grown-up and how they can help.
- You can use "I" statements to ask for what you want.
- You can set boundaries for yourself at home, in social situations, and online.

Knowledge is power, and you've got a lot to help you and to share with others. How empowering!

FEELING FABULOUS

Part of being human means you'll feel uncertain through-out life, and you may continue to wonder who you are as you grow up. We all wonder! The beautiful thing about life is that it is always changing and giving us the chance to be the best version of ourselves with each new day. Remember that your sister, brother, friend, classmates— even parents—are going through their own changes, and sometimes the way people feel or act has nothing to do with you or your relationship with them.

Remember, these changes and strong emotions aren't as powerful as your strength and confidence. Everything you're feeling is normal, and we've learned that there are healthy and unhealthy ways of managing it all. Using your favorite tricks to manage emotions is the best way to grow up great, like talking it out when you get into a fight with a friend or reminding yourself to take a few deep breaths when you're mad.

You might run into different kinds of situations not mentioned in this book that cause you to feel worried, jealous, excited, or disappointed. Trust that no matter what happens, you can count on yourself and your favorite tricks to get you through it and keep a positive mindset. You're one fabulous person, and I am so very proud of you!

I FEEL...

Congratulations! You've finished this book and learned so many wonderful things about yourself and your changing emotions as you grow. I hope you feel as proud of yourself as I do of you.

Take a moment to think about your emotions and circle any feelings you have now that you've finished the book:

EXCITED   CAPABLE

UNCERTAIN   SAD

POSITIVE   FEARFUL

HAPPY   JOYFUL

CURIOUS   CONFIDENT

SILLY   EMBARRASSED

BORED   ANXIOUS

THOUGHTFUL   CHEERFUL

PROUD

HOPEFUL

MAD

STRONG

CALM

SURPRISED

OPTIMISTIC

SHY

GRATEFUL

COMFORTABLE

FRUSTRATED

NERVOUS

EMPOWERED

WORRIED

SAFE

SERIOUS

Think of your own and add them here:

_____

_____

Remember, you can always come back to this book to keep what you've learned fresh. The more you use these tips and tricks, the better you will start to feel.

RESOURCES

Here are some resources for you and your parents or other trusted adults to explore together to learn more about emotions, puberty, and just growing up great!

Print Books

Girls in Real Life Situations: Group Counseling Activities for Enhancing Social and Emotional Development, by Julia V. Taylor and Shannon Trice-Black

This book has so many great activities to promote social skills. It can be used both inside and outside the classroom and is easy to understand.

The Self-Compassion Workbook for Teens, by Karen Bluth, PhD

This workbook helps you progress in loving yourself in fun, interactive ways on every page. It's a book you can write in and use every day to remember to be kind to yourself, ignore your negative thoughts, and feel proud of who you are.

Being Me: A Kid's Guide to Boosting Confidence and Self-Esteem, by Wendy L. Moss, PhD

There are so many wonderful and relatable examples of self-esteem and self-confidence in this book that are sure to help any child, confident or not. This book offers tools for dealing with low self-esteem and helps children grow this confidence in any circumstance.

Online Resources

Always remember to ask for permission before using the Internet or downloading any apps.

Your Life Your Voice

yourlifeyourvoice.org

A great place to find everything you need in a crisis or when you feel like you have no one to talk to. It has numbers for hotlines or text lines, a Q&A section, and a "Tips & Tools" section.

GirlsHealth.Gov

girlshealth.gov

This site lets you explore everything in your life from friendship drama to the proper nutrition you should be getting, and even things that aren't talked about as often, like illnesses and disabilities, or environmental stuff like how to help take care of the planet.

A Mighty Girl

amightygirl.com

Find tons of age-appropriate recommendations for books, TV, movies, toys, and clothing. The website describes itself as "the world's largest collection of books, toys, and movies for smart, confident, and courageous girls." It sounds like a pretty awesome place!

Amy Poehler's Smart Girls YouTube Channel

youtube.com/user/smartgirls

This channel is designed for curious, smart girls like you. It has videos about everything from "modern texting manners" and making math fun, to interviews with amazing women like famous astronaut Dr. Jeanette Epps. The channel is catered a bit more toward older girls, so be sure to ask for permission before watching.

REFERENCES

MY CHANGING EMOTIONS

American Psychological Association. "Stress Effects on the Body." Accessed February 23, 2020. apa.org /helpcenter/stress-body.

Bailey, Regina. "The Limbic System of the Brain: The Amygdala, Hypothalamus, and Thalamus." *ThoughtCo.* Last modified March 28, 2018. thoughtco .com/limbic-system-anatomy-373200.

Bergland, Christopher. "Mindfulness Made Simple." *Psychology Today.* March 31, 2013. psychologytoday.com/us/blog/the-athletes -way/201303/mindfulness-made-simple.

Brain Made Simple. "Hypothalamus." Last modified November 13, 2019. brainmadesimple.com /hypothalamus.

BrightFocus Foundation. "Brain Anatomy and Limbic System." Last modified July 21, 2019. brightfocus .org/alzheimers/infographic/brain-anatomy -and-limbic-system.

Cherry, Kendra. "The 6 Types of Basic Emotions and Their Effect on Human Behavior." *Verywell Mind.* Last modified January 13, 2020. verywellmind.com /an-overview-of-the-types-of-emotions-4163976.

CHOC Children's Hospital. "Sleep Hygiene for Children." Accessed February 23, 2020. choc.org/wp /wp-content/uploads/2016/04/Sleep-Hygiene -Children-Handout.pdf.

Dusenbery, Maya. "How Exercise Affects 2 Important 'Happy' Chemicals in Your Brain." *Livestrong.com.* Last modified October 18, 2019. livestrong.com/article/25 1785-exercise-and-its-effects-on-serotonin-dopamine -levels.

Halloran, Janine. "Deep Breathing Exercises for Kids." *Coping Skills for Kids.* Accessed February 23, 2020. copingskillsforkids.com/deep-breathing -exercises-for-kids.

Healthy Brains. "6 Pillars of Brain Health." Accessed February 23, 2020. healthybrains.org/pillar-physical.

Immordino-Yang, Mary Helen, and Vanessa Singh. "Hippocampal Contributions to the Processing of Social Emotions." *Human Brain Mapping* 34, no. 4 (October 2011): 945–55. doi.org/10.1002/hbm.21485.

Komninos, Andreas. "Our Three Brains—The Emotional Brain." *Interaction Design Foundation.* 2018. interaction-design.org/literature/article/our-three -brains-the-emotional-brain.

Lenzen, Manuela. "Feeling Our Emotions." *Scientific American.* April 1, 2005. scientificamerican.com /article/feeling-our-emotions.

MacMillan, Amanda. "Sleep Tips for Kids of All Ages." *WebMD.* November 23, 2015. webmd.com /parenting/raising-fit-kids/recharge/features /kids-sleep-tips#1.

Moawad, Heidi. "How the Brain Processes Emotions." *Neurology Times.* June 5, 2017. neurologytimes.com /blog/how-brain-processes-emotions.

Pillay, Srini. "How Simply Moving Benefits Your Mental Health." *Harvard Health Blog.* March 28, 2016. health .harvard.edu/blog/how-simply-moving-benefits -your-mental-health-201603289350.

Ramanathan, Mangalam. "Hormones and Chemicals Linked with Our Emotion." *Amrita Vishwa Vidyapeetham.* October 15, 2018. amrita.edu/news /hormones-and-chemicals-linked-our-emotion.

Thomas, David. "Don't Let Your Hippocampus Stop You from Being a Successful Investor." *Forbes Magazine.* May 10, 2018. forbes.com/sites /greatspeculations/2018/05/10/dont-let-your -hippocampus-stop-you-from-being-a-successful -investor/#3faff97d2694.

Young Diggers. "The Fight or Flight Response: Our Body's Response to Stress." February 2010. youngdiggers.com.au/fight-or-flight.

MY CHANGING MIND

Blakemore, Sarah-Jayne, Stephanie Burnett, and Ronald E. Dahl. "The Role of Puberty in the Developing Adolescent Brain." *Human Brain Mapping* 31, no. 6 (June 2010): 926–33. doi.org/10.1002/hbm .21052.

Coltrera, Francesca. "Anxiety in Children." *Harvard Health Blog*. August 14, 2018. health.harvard.edu /blog/anxiety-in-children-2018081414532#.

Ehmke, Rachel. "Helping Children Deal with Grief." *Child Mind Institute*. Accessed February 29, 2020. childmind.org/article/helping-children -deal-grief.

Hawkins, Nicole. "Battling Our Bodies: Under-standing and Overcoming Negative Body Images." *Center for Change*. Last modified August 2014. centerforchange.com/battling-bodies-understanding -overcoming-negative-body-images.

Jacobson, Rae. "How to Help Kids Deal with Embarrassment." *Child Mind Institute*. Accessed February 28, 2020. childmind.org/article/help -kids-deal-embarrassment.

KidCentral TN. "Social and Emotional Development: Ages 8-10." Accessed February 27, 2020. kidcentraltn .com/development/8-10-years/social-and-emotional -development-ages-8-10.html.

Rochat, Philippe. "Five Levels of Self-Awareness as They Unfold Early in Life." *Consciousness and Cognition* 12, no. 4 (December 2003): 717-31. doi.org/10.1016/S1053-8100(03)00081-3.

MY CHANGING RELATIONSHIPS

Brotherson, Sean, Divya Saxena, and Geoffrey Zehnacker. "Talking to Children About Peer Pressure." *North Dakota State University*. October 2017. ag.ndsu.edu/publications/kids-family/talking-to-children-about-peer-pressure#section-3.

GirlsHealth.gov. "Friendships." Last modified November 2, 2015. girlshealth.gov/relationships/friendships.

Kennedy-Moore, Eileen. "Children's Growing Friendships." *Psychology Today*. February 26, 2012. psychologytoday.com/us/blog/growing-friendships/201202/childrens-growing-friendships.

MediaSmarts. "Internet Safety Tips by Age: 8-10." January 19, 2017. mediasmarts.ca/tipsheet/internet-safety-tips-age-8-10.

Smith, Leonie. "8 Year Olds On Social Media—What Parents Should Know." *The Cyber Safety Lady*. October 25, 2018. thecybersafetylady.com.au/2018/10/8-year-olds-on-social-media-what-parents-should-know.

Society for Adolescent Health and Medicine. "Mental Health Resources for Adolescents and Young Adults. Accessed March 8, 2020. adolescenthealth.org /Resources/Clinical-Care-Resources/Mental-Health /Mental-Health-Resources-For-Adolesc.aspx.

INDEX

ACKNOWLEDGMENTS

Researching this book has been both refreshing and humbling. I learned a thing or two about myself in the process and feel thankful to have been given this opportunity. This would not have been possible without those in my life who have pushed me out of my comfort zone toward the tough but necessary self-reflection required for this exciting book. Additionally, I am thankful for my dog, Goose, who is always by my side.

Last but certainly not least, thank you to all the young girls I've had the pleasure of working with and learning from. You've taught me so much about the beautiful journey you are on, and it has been a privilege to witness. You are all an inspiration to me and to each other, and I hope you see that.

ABOUT THE AUTHOR

LAUREN RIVERS is a resident clinical mental health counselor specializing in child and adolescent mental health. Lauren works at a private practice clinic that specializes in play, art, and sand-tray therapy, and she is trained in eye movement desensitization and reprocessing (EMDR) and neurofeedback training. Lauren received her master's from Johns Hopkins University and worked in outpatient settings throughout the city and county of Baltimore.

In addition, Lauren is vice president of a nonprofit organization, Wings of Joanne, that provides respite care and entertainment to bedridden pediatric patients and their families through virtual reality and gaming consoles. Lauren knows the importance of the psychosocial well-being of these children and their families and presented on this topic at Princeton University in 2019.

She resides in Northern Virginia and enjoys exploring the greater DC area, but frequently takes trips home to spend time with her family on the beaches of Alabama and Florida. You can learn more about her interests and passions at LaurenRiversTherapy.com and WingsOfJoanne.com.

NOTES

NOTES

NOTES

NOTES

NOTES